UNBELIEVABOWL
Paleo

UNBELIEVA**BOWL** *Paleo*

60

Wholesome One-Dish Recipes You Won't Believe
Are Dairy- and Gluten-Free

KELSEY PRECIADO

founder of Little Bits of Real Food

PAGE STREET
PUBLISHING CO.

PAGE STREET
PUBLISHING CO.

Dedication

To my husband Matt, this book would not exist without your constant support, love and taste testing! You give me the confidence to do anything I set my mind to and this book is no exception. Love you!

Contents

Introduction

Wow, this book is finally in your hands! I have been dreaming for years of the moment you would read these words, and I hope you are about to fall in love with this cookbook.

From a young age, I loved cooking and everything that comes with it. I love experimenting with flavor combinations and remaking dishes I eat at restaurants. But my favorite part about cooking is watching the faces of the people I feed. Watching my mom try my Paleo banana bread to see her shocked reaction that something so healthy could taste good, or watching my husband's eyes basically roll to the back of his head when I've made another garlicky potato dish he can't get enough of—those are the best moments for me.

Those moments are the reason I decided to start my blog eight years ago. It began as a hobby and a way to share recipes with friends and family, and slowly but surely over time, it turned into my full-time career. I couldn't be happier about that! Sharing healthy, mostly Paleo recipes helped get me on *The Dr. Oz Show*, featured in magazines such as *Glamour*, as well as a ton of your favorite websites such as BuzzFeed and People.com. Creating a space on the internet for people to come to when they want some food inspiration or just a laugh has been such an honor—and now I get to do it in print! It is my extreme privilege to give you the chance to wow your friends, family and yourself with some seriously delicious Paleo bowls.

Paleo bowls was a concept I thought of because they are the dishes that I make for most meals. I always have some veggies, protein and sauce in the fridge, and I end up throwing them all together for a delicious meal that the whole family loves. Bowls are my go-to meal because they are delicious and because they come together quickly! You will notice that in most of these recipes, you will either be cooking your meat in the oven while your veggies cook on the stovetop, or everything cooks up on the stove in less than 30 minutes. These meals also work well when everything mixes together and are great for making ahead: just store each meal in individual containers and take them on the go or to work. These are the kind of meals that I need as a busy mom!

When people ask me how I maintain a healthy lifestyle, my answer is simple: I make healthy food taste incredible. In this book, I put together meals that satisfy on warm days, cold days and, of course, those days when you need something sweet! If you love a crispy chicken nugget, my Crispy Cashew & Coconut Chicken Popper Bowl (page 24) will solve all of your problems. Have a hankering for pasta? The Sweet Potato Carbonara (page 20) will knock your carbalicious socks off.

Sticking with a health journey should be completely enjoyable or it will be impossible to maintain, and that's where I come in. I want all of us to be a bunch of eighty-five-year-olds, skipping around town one day with everyone asking us, "HOW?!" And we will say, "Well, I ate a clean and healthy diet—and I really enjoyed life too."

I mean WOW. I stock my fridge and pantry with veggies, fruit, meat and nuts, and I also fully enjoy my wine and pizza nights when I want them. That is called food freedom, people. The best part? You can do this too! Everyone is on their own journey and finds their own unique way to feel their best. I'm just here to help you see that you might be surprised at how unbelieva-bowl a healthy Paleo meal can be when you have the right recipe!

Throughout the book you will find recipes for rice made out of vegetables, cheese made out of nuts and a crazy good cake made from root flour. Sound a little too healthy for you? TRUST! Trust that my love for food and flavor would never let you down. Now dive into this book with an open mind and an open mouth.

Kelsey Preciado

Nutritious & Nostalgic

We all have a soft spot for the food we grew up eating. Food is always pretty comforting, but when you eat something you had when you were a kid, it can give you all the warm and fuzzy feelings! There are a few recipes that I make that immediately take me back to a certain moment in time. Some of the recipes in this chapter remind me of home or college, but all of them give me that sense of nostalgia and excitement.

Most "memory foods" are covered in cheese or deep fried though, right?! They are foods you had before you really started caring about what you put in your body. But that doesn't mean they have to stay like that! The key is using veggies instead of heavy carbs and cashews instead of cheese—hello, Philly Cheesesteak Bowls (page 15). The meals in this chapter are packed with nutrients, but not packed with regret. They'll give you all the sentimental feelings and leave you satisfied and full of energy, too.

PHILLY CHEESESTEAK BOWLS

Serves 4

There was a small Philly cheesesteak place in my college town that had the most amazing sandwiches. I was obsessed with smothering mine in ketchup—one of my fave foods—and I was so sad when they closed. Now that I don't opt for those kinds of sandwiches much anymore, I have found the beauty in actually being able to taste meat without it being coated in bread and cheese! These bowls are a fabulous Paleo take on my favorite kind of Philly cheesesteak.

Sauce

1 cup (140 g) raw cashews

½ cup plus 2 tbsp (150 ml) water

1 tbsp (6 g) nutritional yeast

½ tsp garlic powder

1 tsp salt

Veggies

3 tbsp (45 ml) avocado or olive oil, divided

4 cups (400 g) cauliflower rice

1 tbsp (15 ml) water

½ tsp garlic powder

1 small red onion, thinly sliced

2 bell peppers, thinly sliced in strips

2 cups (192 g) sliced button mushrooms

1 cup (240 g) canned, diced, fire-roasted tomatoes, drained

Salt and pepper

Meat

1 lb (454 g) sirloin steak, thinly sliced★

1 tsp salt

½ tsp pepper

2 tbsp (30 ml) avocado or olive oil

Sauce

In a blender, combine the cashews, water, nutritional yeast, garlic powder and salt. Blend on high until smooth. Set it aside.

Veggies

Place a large skillet over medium heat and pour 1 tablespoon (15 ml) of oil in the pan. Once the pan is hot, add the cauliflower rice and cook, stirring occasionally, for 5 minutes. Add 2 tablespoons (30 ml) of the sauce and the water to the cauliflower rice. Stir to combine. Add the garlic powder and set it aside.

Place another large skillet over medium heat and pour in 2 tablespoons (30 ml) of oil. Once the pan is hot, add the onion, bell peppers and mushrooms to the pan and cook for 8 minutes, stirring occasionally. Add the tomatoes and cook for 2 minutes. Season with salt and pepper. Set it aside.

Meat

Place a separate pan over medium heat and let it heat up. In a medium bowl, combine the sirloin steak, salt, pepper and oil. Once the pan is warm, add the steak and cook for 2 minutes, stirring constantly, until the beef is no longer pink.

To assemble the bowls, divide the cauliflower rice among four bowls and top each with sautéed veggies, steak and a drizzle of the cashew cheese sauce.

★ To easily slice the steak, place it in the freezer for 30 minutes and use a serrated bread knife to slice it!

PERFECT MEATLOAF & MASHED POTATO BOWL

Serves 4

When I was growing up, my mom had a few dishes on rotation that we all loved. Her meatloaf was incredible because she soaked bread in milk and then tore it up and added it to the mix. I thought no Paleo meatloaf could come close but, my friends, it happened! Even my mom is in love with this recipe, and I know it's going to become a staple in your house just like it is in mine now.

Meatloaf

1 tbsp (15 ml) avocado or olive oil

½ onion, chopped

1 tsp dried oregano

1 tsp salt

½ tsp pepper

2 tbsp (30 ml) coconut aminos

¼ cup (60 ml) beef or chicken broth

1 tbsp (16 g) tomato paste

½ lb (226 g) ground beef

½ lb (226 g) ground pork

¼ cup (37 g) almond flour

1 egg

Ketchup

⅓ cup (87 g) tomato paste

2 tbsp (30 ml) maple syrup

½ tsp garlic powder

½ tsp onion powder

2 tsp (10 ml) coconut aminos

1 tbsp (15 ml) apple cider vinegar

¼ tsp salt

2 tbsp (30 ml) water

Mashed Potatoes

4 medium russet potatoes, peeled and chopped

⅓ cup (80 ml) coconut milk

3 tbsp (42 g) ghee

1 tsp garlic powder

Salt and pepper

Meatloaf

Preheat the oven to 350°F (175°C, or gas mark 4) and line a baking sheet with foil. Place a skillet over medium heat, and pour in the oil and add the onion. Cook for 5 to 7 minutes, or until the onion is translucent and lightly browned. Add the oregano, salt, pepper, coconut aminos, broth and tomato paste. Whisk until combined and cook for 1 minute, then remove it from the heat and let it cool.

In a large bowl, combine the beef, pork, almond flour and egg. Once the onion mixture has cooled slightly, add it to the meat mixture and mix until combined. Make sure not to overmix. Place the meat on the baking sheet and shape it into an 8 x 4–inch (20 x 10–cm) loaf.

Ketchup

In a small bowl, combine the tomato paste, maple syrup, garlic powder, onion powder, coconut aminos, apple cider vinegar and salt. Scoop 3 tablespoons (45 ml) of ketchup on top of the meatloaf and spread it to coat the top. To the remaining ketchup, add 2 tablespoons (30 ml) of water, stir and set it aside.

Place the meatloaf in the oven and bake for 35 to 40 minutes. Let it cool for 10 minutes, then slice it into 8 pieces.

Mashed Potatoes

While the meatloaf is in the oven, bring a large pot of water to a boil. Add a large pinch of salt to the water, then add the potatoes. Boil for 10 minutes, or until fork tender. Remove the potatoes and place them in a food processor. Add the coconut milk, ghee and garlic powder. Blend on high for 1 to 2 minutes, or until smooth. Season to taste with salt and pepper, then blend again.

Scoop mashed potatoes into each bowl. Top with two slices of meatloaf and drizzle on the reserved ketchup.

Prep Ahead: Ketchup can be made up to 1 week in advance and kept in the fridge. The meatloaf is best if cooked fresh, but you can make it up to 4 days ahead of time and reheat it in the oven at 350°F (175°C, or gas mark 4) for 10 minutes.

CHEESE-LESS CHICKEN PARM BOWL   Serves 4

Another staple in our house growing up was chicken Parmesan. The flavors now bring me all kinds of nostalgia and when panfried chicken is swimming in marinara, I am a happy girl. So, this bowl was created, and it is filled with that classic flavor and coated with a dairy-free Parmesan that is sure to become a fridge necessity from now on.

Dairy-Free Parmesan
⅓ cup (47 g) raw cashews
3 tbsp (18 g) nutritional yeast
½ tsp garlic powder
½ tsp onion powder
½ tsp salt

Meat
1 lb (454 g) chicken tenders
Salt and pepper
1 egg
¾ cup (170 g) cassava flour★
2 tsp (6 g) garlic powder
1 tsp dried oregano
1 tsp dried basil
1 tsp salt
¼ cup (60 ml) avocado or olive oil
1 cup (240 ml) marinara sauce

Veggies
1 tbsp (15 ml) avocado or olive oil
1 lb (454 g) butternut squash noodles
Salt
1 cup (240 ml) marinara sauce
¼ cup (10 g) chopped fresh basil

Dairy-Free Parmesan
In a food processor, combine the cashews, nutritional yeast, garlic powder, onion powder and salt. Pulse just until it resembles fine breadcrumbs. Be sure not to blend too long or it will turn into nut butter!

Meat
Cut each chicken tender into 4 to 5 pieces and sprinkle with salt and pepper. Crack an egg into a bowl and whisk it. In another bowl, combine the cassava flour, garlic powder, oregano, basil and salt. Take each chunk of chicken and dip it in the egg to coat, then in the cassava mixture to coat, then onto a plate. Repeat with the rest of the chicken.

Place a large skillet over medium heat. Once the pan is warm, pour in the oil and allow it to heat up. Place all of the chicken in the pan in one even layer. Cook for 3 minutes per side. Once cooked, remove it from the pan and pour out any remaining oil. Add the marinara sauce to the pan and bring it to a simmer. Add the chicken and let simmer for 2 minutes.

Veggies
While the chicken cooks, place a separate large skillet over medium heat. Pour the oil in the pan. Add the butternut squash noodles and cook for 5 minutes, tossing them as they cook. You want them to be tender but still have some bite. Season to taste with salt, then add the marinara and basil. Toss to coat.

To assemble the bowls, divide the noodles among four bowls. Top each with chicken pieces and a spoonful of marinara, and sprinkle with dairy-free Parmesan.

★ Cassava Flour: This Paleo flour is made from the cassava root. It is a great alternative for breading, because it is nut-free but has a slightly nutty flavor and a smooth texture.

Prep Ahead: Dairy-free Parmesan can be made up to 2 weeks ahead of time and stored in the fridge.

SWEET POTATO CARBONARA   Serves 4

So many food memories come from my college days. There was a pasta place that had the most amazing carbonara that you could get with any kind of pasta, and it was a fast-casual place so we would load up all the time. Important disclaimer: I played water polo in college so carbs = life. I remade this classic with some sweet potato noodles for a lighter take that is free from refined grains, so it won't weigh you down or make you feel sluggish!

4 medium sweet potatoes

2 tbsp (30 ml) avocado or olive oil

4 oz (113 g) pancetta

2 tsp (6 g) minced garlic

2 large eggs plus 1 egg yolk

¼ cup (27 g) nutritional yeast

¼ cup (60 ml) water

1 tsp arrowroot powder

Salt and pepper

1 handful of fresh flat-leaf parsley, chopped

Peel the sweet potatoes, then use a spiralizer to cut them into spaghetti-sized noodles.

Place a large skillet over medium heat and pour the oil in the pan. Add the pancetta and cook for about 3 minutes until crispy, then add the garlic and cook for 1 minute. Add the spiralized sweet potatoes to the pan. Cook, covered, tossing occasionally, for 5 to 8 minutes until the sweet potato noodles are tender.

In a medium bowl, combine the eggs plus the egg yolk and whisk until well blended. Add the nutritional yeast, water and arrowroot powder and whisk again. Remove the sweet potatoes from the heat and place them in a large bowl. Slowly add the egg mixture while tossing them continually to slowly cook the egg.

Once it is all added, season with salt and pepper to taste. Divide among four bowls and top with parsley.

LEMON-ROSEMARY CHICKEN BOWL   Serves 4

The hubby and I are quite a bit obsessed with rosemary. We have been making this lemon-rosemary chicken for years and when I realized that for some reason it wasn't on my blog yet, I knew it was just meant for this cookbook! This recipe includes such an easy, throw-together, stovetop sauce that you will want to coat your life with it. This is a perfect example of a simple Paleo weeknight meal that packs a ton of flavor!

Meat

1 lb (454 g) chicken breasts

1 tsp salt

¼ tsp pepper

1 tbsp (15 ml) avocado or olive oil

Sauce

1 cup (240 ml) chicken broth

¼ cup (60 ml) lemon juice

1 tbsp (2 g) chopped fresh rosemary

½ tsp garlic powder

1 tsp arrowroot powder plus 1 tbsp (15 ml) water

Salt and pepper

Veggies

2 tbsp (30 ml) avocado or olive oil

2 medium russet potatoes, peeled and chopped

2 cups (268 g) chopped asparagus

6 cups (402 g) chopped kale

½ tsp salt, plus more to taste

¼ tsp pepper

½ tsp garlic powder

Meat

Chop the chicken into bite-size pieces and sprinkle the salt and pepper all over them.

Place a skillet over medium heat. Pour in the oil and add the chicken to the pan. Cook the pieces for about 3 minutes per side, or until cooked through. Once cooked, remove the chicken from the pan and set it aside.

Sauce

In the same pan, add the broth, lemon juice, rosemary and garlic powder. Whisk together and bring to a boil, then add the arrowroot mixture and whisk quickly to combine and thicken the sauce. Season with salt and pepper to taste, then add the chicken to coat it with the sauce.

Veggies

Meanwhile, place a separate large skillet over medium heat. Pour the oil in the pan, and once it is warm, add the potatoes. Toss to coat with oil and cook for 10 minutes, stirring occasionally. Add the asparagus to the pan and cook for 5 minutes. Once the potatoes are fork tender, add the kale, salt, pepper and garlic powder. Toss to combine. Cook for 30 seconds to slightly wilt the kale. Season to taste with more salt.

To assemble the bowls, divide the veggies among four bowls and top each with chicken. Spoon on the remaining sauce and enjoy!

CRISPY CASHEW & COCONUT CHICKEN POPPER BOWL

I am a huge Trader Joe's fan, and I love their coconut cashews. They are the reason I realized that this combo is incredible, and why I knew it had to be featured in this book. The flavor combo also makes a great chicken breading so this popper bowl can be crunchy and packed with seasoning all at the same time. You will love the crunch that brings you back to your chicken nugget days!

Meat

½ cup (70 g) raw cashews

½ cup (114 g) shredded coconut

¼ cup (28 g) coconut flour

1 tsp salt

½ tsp pepper

1 lb (454 g) boneless skinless chicken breasts, cubed

1 large egg

Olive oil spray or 2 tbsp (30 ml) olive oil for drizzling

Veggies

1 tbsp (15 ml) avocado or olive oil

8 cups (800 g) cauliflower rice

½ cup (120 ml) coconut milk

1 medium roasted red pepper, finely chopped

1 mango, peeled and finely chopped

½ tsp ground ginger

1 tsp garlic powder

Salt and pepper

Meat

Preheat the oven to 400°F (200°C, or gas mark 6) and line a baking sheet with parchment paper.

In a food processor, combine the cashews, coconut, coconut flour, salt and pepper. Blend on high for 1 to 2 minutes, until it resembles breadcrumbs.

Place the cubed chicken in a medium bowl and crack the egg into the bowl. Mix them together, breaking up the egg to coat the chicken.

Pour the cashew-coconut breadcrumbs in a bowl. One by one, coat each piece of chicken, then place them on the baking sheet. Spray or lightly drizzle the chicken pieces with oil.

Bake for 8 minutes, then flip each piece over and bake for 8 to 10 minutes more, or until lightly browned.

Veggies

Place a large skillet over medium heat and pour the oil in the pan. Add the cauliflower rice and cook for about 5 minutes, stirring occasionally. Add the coconut milk, roasted red pepper, mango, ginger and garlic powder. Stir and cook for 3 to 4 minutes, until the cauliflower rice is tender. Season with salt and pepper to taste.

To assemble the bowls, divide the cauliflower rice among four bowls and top each with some chicken poppers!

BBQ CHICKEN PIZZA BOWL

Serves 4

I've said it before, and I will say it again: BBQ chicken pizza is the best. I know, I know, a "works" pizza or classic margherita are great too, but something about the sweet BBQ sauce with chicken, red onion and cilantro makes my heart so happy.

Meat

1 lb (454 g) chicken breasts

1 tsp salt

¼ tsp pepper

¾ cup (180 ml) Paleo BBQ sauce★, divided

Veggies

5 gold potatoes

3 cups (300 g) cauliflower florets

¼ cup (60 ml) chicken broth

¼ cup (60 ml) coconut milk

¼ tsp liquid smoke

Salt and pepper

¼ cup (40 g) finely chopped red onion

1 tbsp (1 g) chopped cilantro

Meat

Preheat the oven to 400°F (200°C, or gas mark 6). Chop the chicken into bite-size pieces and place them on a parchment paper–lined baking sheet. Sprinkle with salt and pepper. Toss to coat. Bake for 15 minutes. Remove the chicken and toss with ½ cup (120 ml) of BBQ sauce.

Veggies

While the chicken is cooking, bring a large pot of water to a boil. Peel and chop the potatoes and add them to the pot with the cauliflower. Boil for 7 minutes, or until fork tender. Drain the potatoes.

Place the cooked potatoes and cauliflower in a food processor with the broth, coconut milk and liquid smoke. Blend until smooth. Season to taste with salt and pepper.

To assemble the bowls, scoop the potato-cauliflower mixture into four bowls and top each with chicken, some red onion and cilantro. Drizzle on the remaining BBQ sauce.

★ Primal Kitchen makes delicious Paleo BBQ sauces.

Prep Ahead: Cook the chicken and make the veggie mash up to 4 days ahead of time and store separately in the fridge.

CHICKEN PICCATA MEATBALLS WITH ZOODLES Serves 4

Here is a dish that is made so much easier by having a jar of lemon juice on hand at all times. I don't know about you, but I am much too busy to be squeezing lemons at dinnertime. The zip that comes from the lemon juice and capers in a chicken piccata is such a simple concept that brings back all of the memories of my mom making chicken piccata!

Meat

1 lb (454 g) ground chicken

1 egg

½ cup (74 g) almond flour

1 tsp lemon zest

1 tsp garlic powder

1 tsp salt

½ tsp pepper

Sauce

⅓ cup (80 ml) lemon juice

1 cup (240 ml) chicken broth

¼ cup (57 g) brined capers, rinsed

1 tbsp (14 g) ghee

1 tsp arrowroot powder plus 1 tbsp (15 ml) water

Salt and pepper

Veggies

6 medium zucchinis

Meat

Preheat the oven to 400°F (200°C, or gas mark 6) and line a baking sheet with parchment paper.

In a medium bowl, combine the chicken, egg, almond flour, lemon zest, garlic powder, salt and pepper. Once fully combined, scoop into 16 balls and place them on the baking sheet. Wet your hands with water so the chicken doesn't stick to them. Bake the meatballs for 16 minutes, then set them aside in a bowl.

Sauce

Place a large skillet over medium heat. Mix the lemon juice, broth, capers and ghee in the pan. Bring to a simmer, then add the arrowroot mixture and whisk to thicken the sauce for 2 to 3 minutes. Pour all but 2 tablespoons (30 ml) of the sauce over the meatballs.

Veggies

Line a large bowl with paper towels. Use a spiralizer to cut the zucchini into zoodles (zucchini noodles). In the same pan the sauce was made in, cook the zoodles for 5 minutes, tossing constantly to avoid overcooking, until they are tender but still have a bite. Remove the zoodles from the pan and add them to the bowl, leaving any water in the pan. Pour 2 tablespoons (30 ml) of the sauce over the zoodles, and add a little salt and pepper to taste. Stir to combine.

To assemble the bowls, divide the zoodles among four bowls and top with 4 meatballs each.

Prep Ahead: Make the meatballs and sauce, combine the two and keep it in the fridge for up to 4 days in advance.

Fabulously Fresh

I have a few rules for salad if it is going to be a full meal. Rule #1: It must have at least three toppings, but five is preferable. Rule #2: The dressing must be so delicious that you could dip a plain piece of chicken in it and it would taste amazing. And rule #3: It should actually barely qualify as a salad because it's really just a bowl packed with tasty things and one just happens to be greens.

Some of the dishes in here are slaws, which I love because they are a salad that lasts a few days after being dressed! The great thing about salads in a Paleo-based diet is that there are a ton of Paleo ingredients to add texture and flavor to a bowl. Nuts and seeds are my favorite way to top these bowls because of the crunch factor. I also love to add fruit to a salad bowl. It should be beautiful with everything sprinkled on top. Then when you have taken your Instagram photo, you should be able to mix it all up with a fork and relish in the fact that every bite is a surprise. How pumped are you to make a salad right now?! Go on, friend, do it!

APPLE COBB BOWL

Serves 4

I've said it before, and I will say it again—add bacon and avocado to ANYTHING and you have a winning recipe—especially in the Paleo world! These are just the facts I live my life by, and I think you should too. Add this homemade ranch dressing and you are in healthy food heaven. Oh, and you will probably want to put this dressing on everything, which is understandable and totally allowed!

Meat

4 slices bacon

1 lb (454 g) boneless skinless chicken breasts

Salt and pepper

Dressing

¾ cup (180 ml) light olive oil

1 egg

½ tsp mustard powder

2 tbsp (30 ml) lemon juice

1 tbsp (3 g) chopped fresh dill

2 tbsp (8 g) chopped fresh parsley

½ tsp garlic powder

¼ cup (60 ml) light coconut milk

Salt and pepper

Veggies & Fruit

1 head of romaine, chopped

2 medium Fuji apples, peeled and chopped

4 large hard–boiled eggs, chopped

1 cup (149 g) cherry tomatoes, chopped

1 avocado, pitted and chopped

Meat

Place a large skillet over medium heat and let it warm up. Place the bacon in the pan and cook for about 3 minutes, until crispy, flipping halfway through the cooking time. Remove the bacon from the pan but keep the bacon fat in the pan.

Sprinkle both sides of the chicken breasts with salt and pepper and add them to the bacon fat in the pan. Cook the chicken for 4 minutes per side, or until cooked through. Remove and let it rest for 5 minutes. Chop the chicken and bacon. Set them aside.

Dressing

In an immersion blender cup, combine the oil, egg, mustard powder, lemon juice, dill, parsley, garlic powder and coconut milk. Place the immersion blender at the bottom of the cup and turn it on for about 30 seconds, or until the dressing starts to thicken at the bottom. Slowly move the immersion blender up the cup to thicken the rest of the ranch dressing. Once it is done, season with salt and pepper to taste.

Veggies & Fruit

In a large bowl, place the romaine and drizzle it with your desired amount of ranch dressing. Toss to coat the lettuce.

Divide the lettuce evenly into four bowls and top each with the bacon, chicken, apples, hard–boiled eggs, cherry tomatoes and avocado.

Prep Ahead: Cook the bacon and chicken up to 4 days ahead of time and store them in the fridge. Make the dressing up to 2 weeks ahead of time and store it in the fridge. The lettuce and cherry tomatoes can be chopped up to 3 days ahead of time as well.

TENDER BEEF MEATBALLS WITH CAESAR SLAW

Serves 4

It is my firm belief that everyone needs a solid Paleo beef meatball recipe in their repertoire. This one can be yours! It is simple, full of flavor and has ground fennel and garlic powder—which I think you should always have in your cabinet anyways. The meatballs are so tender, and they pair perfectly with the creamy crunch of the slaw!

Meat

1 lb (454 g) ground beef

¼ cup (37 g) almond flour

1 large egg

1 tsp ground fennel

1 tsp garlic powder

½ tsp oregano

1 tbsp (15 ml) Dijon mustard

1 tsp salt

¼ tsp pepper

Veggies

4 cups (268 g) shredded kale

3 cups (210 g) shredded green cabbage

3 cups (210 g) shredded red cabbage

2 cups (220 g) shredded carrots

Caesar Dressing

⅓ cup (78 g) mayonnaise★

¼ cup (60 ml) avocado or olive oil

½ tsp garlic powder

2 tbsp (30 ml) fresh lemon juice

2 tsp (10 ml) coconut aminos

1 tsp Dijon mustard

1 tsp nutritional yeast

1 tsp anchovy paste

Salt and pepper

Meat

Preheat the oven to 350°F (175°C, or gas mark 4). Line a baking sheet with foil.

In a medium bowl, combine the beef, almond flour, egg, fennel, garlic powder, oregano, Dijon mustard, salt and pepper. Mix with a wooden spoon or your hands until evenly combined. Scoop into 16 meatballs. Place the meatballs on the baking sheet and bake for 16 minutes.

Veggies

In a large bowl, combine the kale, cabbages and carrots.

Caesar Dressing

In a small bowl, combine the mayonnaise, oil, garlic powder, lemon juice, coconut aminos, Dijon mustard, nutritional yeast and anchovy paste. Whisk to combine thoroughly, and season to taste with salt and pepper.

Pour the sauce over the slaw and mix to evenly coat. Divide among four bowls and top with the meatballs.

★ Mayonnaise: When I use mayo in this book, I am always using an avocado oil–based mayonnaise with clean ingredients. There are a lot of mayonnaise options now, but the ingredients are so important here for it to be Paleo. My favorite brand is Primal Kitchen.

Prep Ahead: Make the meatballs and chop the veggies up to 4 days ahead of time and store them separately in the fridge. Make the dressing up to 2 weeks ahead of time and store it in the fridge.

LOADED GREEK LUNCH BOWL

Serves 4

I have a big love affair with tahini. Really, all Mediterranean food and the sauces that come with it hold a large place in my heart! I had to hold myself back from making most of this book a combination of Greek-inspired bowls because this tahini sauce is just too good. So, I just put all of the good stuff in this recipe so you can make it at least once a week like we do.

Meat

1 lb (454 g) boneless, skinless chicken thighs

2 tbsp (30 ml) lemon juice

1 tsp garlic powder

½ tsp dried oregano

1 tsp salt

¼ tsp pepper

2 tbsp (30 ml) avocado or olive oil

Veggies

1 head of romaine lettuce, chopped

2 cups (298 g) chopped cherry tomatoes

2 cups (208 g) chopped cucumber

¼ cup (15 g) chopped fresh parsley

1 tsp chopped mint

½ cup (27 g) chopped Kalamata olives

2 tbsp (30 ml) avocado or olive oil

1 tbsp (15 ml) red wine vinegar

Pinch of salt

Lemon-Herb Tahini Sauce

¼ cup (60 ml) tahini

2 tbsp (30 ml) lemon juice

3 tbsp (45 ml) water

½ tsp garlic powder

1 tbsp (3 g) finely chopped fresh parsley

1 tsp finely chopped dill

½ tsp finely chopped mint

Salt

Meat

Cut the chicken thighs into 1-inch (2.5-cm) cubes, then place them in a large glass dish. Sprinkle the lemon juice, garlic powder, dried oregano, salt and pepper over the chicken, then mix so the chicken is evenly coated. Let the chicken marinate for about 5 minutes as you preheat a large skillet over medium heat.

Pour the oil in the skillet and allow it to warm up. Add the chicken with tongs so you don't pour the excess liquid from the marinade into the pan. Cook for 3 to 4 minutes per side, or until the chicken is cooked through. Remove the chicken and set it aside.

Veggies

In a large bowl, combine the romaine lettuce, cherry tomatoes, cucumber, parsley, mint, olives, oil and vinegar. Toss to coat the veggies, then season with just a pinch of salt.

Sauce

In a small bowl, combine the tahini, lemon juice, water, garlic powder, parsley, dill and mint. Stir to combine and season to taste with salt.

Divide the veggie mixture into four bowls and top each with one-quarter of the chicken. Drizzle each bowl with the desired amount of tahini sauce.

Prep Ahead: Cook or pre-marinate the chicken and chop the veggies up to 4 days ahead of time. The sauce can be made up to 2 weeks ahead of time and stored in the fridge. Tahini seizes up in the fridge so when you are ready to serve, thin the sauce out slightly with water, adding it 1 tablespoon (15 ml) at a time until your desired consistency is achieved.

CHIPOTLE-LIME CHICKEN SALAD   Serves 4

I wasn't raised with too much spice in the house, so I really started using chipotle seasoning after college. I still can't handle much heat, but the flavor of chipotle is a family favorite! It pairs so well with lime and all of the crunchy toppings to give this Paleo salad a one-two punch.

Meat
1 lb (454 g) boneless, skinless chicken thighs

2 tbsp (30 ml) avocado or olive oil, divided

½ tsp chipotle powder

1 tbsp (15 ml) lime juice

1 tsp garlic powder

½ tsp onion powder

1 tsp salt

¼ tsp pepper

Veggies
2 heads of romaine lettuce

1 cup (149 g) chopped cherry tomatoes

½ cup (65 g) chopped jicama

1 medium (136 g) avocado, sliced

¼ cup (35 g) roasted and salted pepitas

Dressing
¼ cup (60 ml) avocado or olive oil

2 tbsp (30 ml) lime juice

¼ tsp chipotle powder

½ tsp garlic powder

1 tbsp (1 g) chopped cilantro

Salt and pepper

Meat
Place the chicken thighs in a glass dish. In a small bowl, combine 1 tablespoon (15 ml) of oil, chipotle powder, lime juice, garlic powder, onion powder, salt and pepper. Rub the spice mixture on the chicken thighs and let them marinate for about 30 minutes.

Place a large skillet over medium heat and let the pan heat up. Pour 1 tablespoon (15 ml) of oil into the pan, then add the chicken thighs. Cook for 4 minutes per side until cooked through, then remove it from the heat and let the chicken cool. Chop the chicken into bite-size pieces.

Veggies
In a large bowl, combine the lettuce, cherry tomatoes, jicama, avocado and pepitas.

Dressing
In a jar with a lid, combine the oil, lime juice, chipotle powder, garlic powder and cilantro. Cover the jar and shake until combined. Season with salt and pepper to taste. Pour the dressing over the veggies and toss to combine.

To assemble the bowls, divide the salad among four bowls and top with the chicken.

Prep Ahead: Cook the chicken, chop the veggies and make the dressing, storing all three things separately in the fridge up to 4 days before eating. Leave out the avocado until you're ready to eat!

SUPERFOOD SALMON BOWL

Serves 4

What are superfoods anyways? Technically superfood is just a marketing term, but it basically means ingredients that pack a punch of nutrition. This bowl is filled with nutritionally-dense ingredients that will keep you satiated for hours. I particularly love keeping a bag of hemp hearts in my fridge to add to salads because they are packed with essential fatty acids.

Veggies

2½ cups (333 g) chopped sweet potatoes
1½ cups (204 g) chopped beets
1 tbsp (15 ml) avocado or olive oil
½ tsp salt
¼ tsp pepper

Meat

1 lb (454 g) salmon fillets
Salt and pepper

Dressing

3 tbsp (45 ml) apple cider vinegar
1 tbsp (15 ml) honey
3 tbsp (45 ml) olive oil
¼ tsp cardamom
⅛ tsp ground ginger
Salt and pepper

Toppings

1 (10-oz [286-g]) bag chopped kale, stems removed
2 tbsp (22 g) pomegranate seeds
1 tbsp (9 g) shelled sunflower seeds
2 tsp (7 g) hemp hearts

Veggies & Meat

Preheat the oven to 400°F (200°C, or gas mark 6). Line a baking sheet with parchment paper. Spread the sweet potatoes and beets on the sheet and toss with the oil, salt and pepper.

Bake the veggies for 25 minutes, then toss them and push them to one side of the sheet. Add the salmon to the pan and sprinkle it with a pinch of salt and pepper. Bake for 15 minutes, until the sweet potatoes are fork tender and the salmon is cooked through.

Dressing

In a jar with a lid, combine the apple cider vinegar, honey, oil, cardamom and ginger. Put the lid on the jar and shake vigorously to combine. Season with salt and pepper to taste.

In a large bowl, pour the dressing over the kale and massage the kale to slightly wilt it and coat it with the dressing.

Divide the kale among four bowls and top each bowl with one-quarter of the salmon, pomegranate seeds, sunflower seeds and hemp hearts.

Prep Ahead: Roast the sweet potatoes and beets up to 4 days ahead of time and store them in the fridge. Make the dressing up to 2 weeks ahead of time and store it in the fridge. Salmon is best prepared just before eating, but if you need to prep ahead you can cook it up to 2 days before.

CHINESE CHICKEN SLAW   Serves 4

This salad is all about ease. My favorite part of a slaw-based salad is that it actually lasts for a few days in the fridge! If you want it to be super crunchy, dress it right before you serve, but if you want the cabbage to soften a little bit, this is great to prep ahead and enjoy once the cabbage is nice and marinated!

Meat
1 lb (454 g) boneless, skinless chicken breasts

¼ cup (60 ml) coconut aminos

1 tsp salt

¼ tsp pepper

1 tsp garlic powder

½ tsp ground ginger

2 tbsp (30 ml) avocado or olive oil

Dressing
½ cup (120 ml) coconut aminos

3 tbsp (45 ml) red wine vinegar

2 tbsp (30 ml) Dijon mustard

⅓ cup (80 ml) avocado or olive oil

1 tbsp (15 ml) toasted sesame oil

Veggies
½ head of green cabbage, thinly sliced

¼ head of red cabbage, thinly sliced

1 cup (110 g) shredded carrots

⅓ cup (5 g) minced fresh cilantro

¼ cup (6 g) fresh basil leaves, thinly sliced

1 cup (100 g) thinly sliced scallions (green and white parts), divided

¼ cup (113 g) toasted sesame seeds

Meat
In a glass dish or plastic bag, combine the chicken breasts, coconut aminos, salt, pepper, garlic powder and ginger. Mix everything to coat the chicken and let sit in the fridge for at least 30 minutes or up to 3 days.

Once marinated, place a large skillet over medium heat and pour the oil in the pan. Place the chicken in the pan and cook for 4 minutes per side, or until the internal temperature is 165°F (74°C). Set it aside.

Dressing
In a jar with a lid, combine the coconut aminos, vinegar, Dijon mustard, oil and toasted sesame oil. Place the lid on the jar and shake it until the dressing is combined.

Veggies
In a large bowl, combine the green cabbage, red cabbage, carrots, cilantro, basil and scallions. Pour the dressing over the top and stir to completely coat all of the veggies. Add the toasted sesame seeds and toss again.

Divide the slaw among four bowls and top with chicken.

Prep Ahead: Cook or marinate the chicken and chop the veggies up to 3 days ahead of time and store in the fridge separately. Make the dressing up to 2 weeks ahead of time and store in the fridge.

JERK-SPICED CHICKEN & AVOCADO SALAD

Serves 4

I may have googled "how jerk seasoning got its name" hoping it was named after someone who wasn't very nice. That is not the case, unfortunately. It actually comes from a Spanish word for jerked or dried meat. Whatever the origin is, jerk seasoning is packed with flavor and is delicious when combined with fresh flavors such as pineapple and lime juice. This salad is great for a summer day and so easy to whip together!

Meat

2 tsp (17 g) jerk seasoning

1 tsp salt

1 lb (454 g) boneless, skinless chicken thighs

3 tbsp (45 ml) avocado or olive oil

Veggies

2 heads of romaine lettuce

1½ cups (248 g) chopped pineapple

¼ cup (40 g) chopped red onion

½ cup (68 g) chopped roasted red pepper

2 medium avocados, pitted and chopped

1 tbsp (1 g) chopped cilantro

1 tbsp (30 ml) lime juice

¼ tsp salt

Dressing

3 tbsp (45 ml) avocado or olive oil

2 tbsp (30 ml) pineapple juice

1 tbsp (15 ml) lime juice

½ tsp garlic powder

¼ tsp jerk seasoning

Salt and pepper

Meat

In a small bowl, combine the jerk seasoning and salt. Sprinkle it over the chicken thighs and rub the seasoning in well. Place a large skillet over medium heat. Once the pan is hot, pour in the oil. Place the chicken in the pan and let it cook without moving it, for 3 minutes. Flip it and cook for 3 to 4 minutes. Remove and let the chicken cool slightly.

Veggies

In a large bowl, add the romaine. In a smaller bowl, combine the pineapple, onion, roasted red pepper, avocados, cilantro, lime juice and salt. Toss to combine.

Dressing

In a jar with a lid, combine the oil, pineapple juice, lime juice, garlic powder and jerk seasoning. Cover the jar and shake it to combine. Season to taste with salt and pepper.

Pour the dressing over the romaine and toss to coat. Divide the romaine among four bowls and top with the jerk chicken and avocado–pineapple salsa.

Prep Ahead: Cook the chicken up to 4 days ahead of time, and make the dressing up to 1 week ahead of time. Store both separately in the fridge.

CREAMY CHIPOTLE-RANCH CHICKEN SALAD   Serves 4

Homemade ranch dressing is something that every Paleo refrigerator should have, but chipotle ranch?! Now that is an absolute must. This recipe features a delicious chipotle ranch that coats chicken and tops a crisp salad for a little bit of everything your taste buds desire. The combination of spice and creaminess makes for a combo that you will crave on a weekly basis!

Meat
1 lb (454 g) boneless, skinless chicken breasts

Salt and pepper

⅔ cup (160 ml) light olive oil

1 large egg

Pinch of mustard powder

1 tbsp (15 ml) lime juice

2 tbsp (3 g) dried parsley

1 tsp chipotle powder

2 tsp (3 g) garlic powder

Veggies
⅓ cup (45 g) chopped roasted red peppers

¼ cup (40 g) minced red onion

1 tbsp (1 g) chopped cilantro

1 tbsp (15 ml) almond milk

2 heads (812 g) romaine lettuce, chopped

1 medium avocado, pitted and chopped

Meat
Preheat the oven to 350°F (175°C, or gas mark 4). Line a baking sheet with parchment paper and place the chicken breasts on top. Sprinkle the chicken with salt and pepper. Bake for 16 to 18 minutes, or until cooked through.

In a large cup or immersion blender cup, combine the oil, egg, mustard powder, lime juice, dried parsley, chipotle powder and garlic powder. Place an immersion blender in the cup, all the way at the bottom and start to blend on medium speed until the ranch becomes white. Slowly move the immersion blender up the cup until the entire mixture is opaque and thick.

When the chicken is cooked, let it cool then chop it into chunks and place them in a bowl. Scoop ½ cup (120 ml) of the chipotle ranch on top of the chicken and toss to coat. Season with salt and pepper to taste.

Veggies
Add the roasted red peppers, onion and cilantro to the chicken salad. Toss to coat.

To the remaining ranch mixture, add the almond milk to thin it slightly.

To assemble the bowls, divide the lettuce into four bowls and top each with one-quarter of the chicken salad mixture. Drizzle each salad with some of the chipotle ranch and top with avocado.

Prep Ahead: Make the chicken salad up to 4 days ahead of time and store in the fridge.

FRESH BEET & BACON BALANCE BOWL

Serves 4

I LOVE alliteration. So this recipe makes me really happy! The name has a lot to do with that, but it's also because this bowl mixes some of my favorite veggies with bacon and drizzles a tahini sauce on top. These are the dishes I live for because you can prep so much of this ahead of time and throw it together for an easy lunch!

Meat
6 slices bacon

Veggies
1 lb (454 g) chopped butternut squash
1 tsp salt
¼ tsp pepper
5 oz (142 g) mixed greens
1 (10-oz [294-g]) can beets

Tahini Sauce
¼ cup (60 ml) tahini
1 tbsp (15 ml) apple cider vinegar
3 tbsp (45 ml) water
½ tsp garlic powder
Salt and pepper

Meat
Place a skillet over medium-high heat and cook the bacon until crispy, about 5 to 7 minutes. Remove and chop, saving the bacon grease for later.

Veggies
Preheat the oven to 400°F (200°C, or gas mark 6). Line a baking sheet with foil and spread the butternut squash over the baking sheet. Pour the reserved bacon grease over the squash and toss to coat. Season with salt and pepper. Roast for 35 to 40 minutes, stirring halfway through the cooking time.

Divide the mixed greens among the bowls. Drain the canned beets and chop them into bite-size pieces. In a medium bowl, combine the roasted butternut squash, beets and bacon. Scoop that mixture over each bowl of greens.

Tahini Sauce
In a small bowl, combine the tahini, apple cider vinegar, water and garlic powder. Stir until smooth, and season with salt and pepper to taste.

Drizzle the tahini sauce over the bowls.

Prep Ahead: Cook the bacon and butternut squash up to 4 days ahead of time, store them in the fridge and reheat on the stovetop. Make the tahini sauce up to 2 weeks ahead of time and store in the fridge. Tahini seizes up in the fridge so when you are ready to serve, thin the sauce out slightly by adding 1 tablespoon (15 ml) of water at a time until your desired consistency is achieved.

SEARED AHI & SESAME MANGO AVOCADO BOWL

Mango and avocado are a match made in my summer dreams! I bet you can agree with me on that—and adding them to kale with a delicious sesame dressing is the perfect side to some seared ahi. Eating this dish feels like you are sitting at a beachside restaurant, and you will be shocked that it's so easy and Paleo!

Meat

1 lb (454 g) ahi tuna

Salt and pepper

1 tbsp (15 ml) sesame oil

Veggies

2 tbsp (30 ml) sesame oil

2 tbsp (30 ml) rice vinegar

½ tsp garlic powder

½ tsp ground ginger

6 cups (402 g) chopped kale

1 mango, chopped

1 avocado, pitted and chopped

4 radishes, sliced

2 cups (298 g) chopped grape tomatoes

1 tsp sesame seeds

Meat

Dry off the tuna with paper towels, then sprinkle both sides with some salt and pepper. Place a large skillet over medium-high heat. Once the pan is hot, pour in the sesame oil. Place the ahi tuna in the pan and sear it for 1½ minutes per side. Set it aside.

Veggies

In a small bowl, combine the sesame oil, rice vinegar, garlic powder and ginger. Whisk to combine. Pour that mixture over the kale and massage it with your hands for 1 minute, or until the leaves are no longer tough. Add the mango, avocado, radishes, grape tomatoes and sesame seeds. Toss to coat.

To serve, divide the salad among four bowls and top each with sliced ahi tuna.

More Delicious than Delivery

After I became a mom, I ordered food delivery more than I like to admit. And ya know what happened each time? I thought, "Wow, I could have made something way better and now I have a stomachache." When we make the recipes in this chapter, Matt (my hubby) and I are always blown away and so impressed with ourselves. All it takes to get there is a good grocery trip at the beginning of the week. I do some chopping during nap time and that sets us up for success.

In my opinion, the best part about takeout food is the sauce. It's usually a bit sweet and absolutely coats the meat—it makes the meal! So in these Paleo bowls, the sauces stand out as they should. In the Sweet Mandarin Chicken with Tri-Veggie Rice (page 64), I used a little bit of honey to naturally sweeten up the sauce, and in the epic Baja Fish Taco Bowl (page 56) there is a creamy slaw that comes together with mayo and lime juice.

The recipes in this chapter, like most in this book, are also designed for the whole family to enjoy. My daughter devoured the filling for the Sesame Chicken Lettuce Wrap Bowl (page 59), and now it is a staple in our routine. So instead of ordering in, thumb through these pages and make something way more delicious that will leave you feeling fantastic!

GARLIC MONGOLIAN BEEF

Serves 4

Three words for you on this one: I LOVE GARLIC. It honestly just makes everything better. We go through garlic powder and minced garlic in my house like nobody's business. So of course, if I am making you a Paleo Mongolian beef recipe, it is going to be stuffed with garlic. Your significant other can thank me later!

Meat

1 lb (454 g) flank steak, thinly sliced into strips

2 tbsp (16 g) arrowroot powder

1 tsp salt

½ tsp pepper

1 tsp garlic powder

3 tbsp (45 ml) avocado or olive oil

1 tbsp (9 g) minced garlic

⅓ cup (80 ml) coconut aminos

¼ cup (60 ml) water

1 tbsp (15 ml) honey

2 scallions, chopped into 1-inch (2.5-cm) strips (green parts only)

Veggies

Tri-Veggie Rice (page 64)

Meat

Place the flank steak in a large plastic bag and pour in the arrowroot powder, salt, pepper and garlic powder. Close the bag and shake it to coat each piece of steak.

Place a large skillet over medium-high heat. Once warm, pour in the oil, then lay out each piece of steak separately so they don't touch. This might take a few batches depending on how big your pan is. Cook the steak for 1 minute per side, then remove it and set it aside.

In the same pan, cook the garlic for 1 minute to soften. Add the coconut aminos, water and honey, and whisk to cook and thicken. The remaining arrowroot in the pan should help thicken the sauce. Cook for about 4 minutes until it has thickened. Add the steak and scallions, and cook for 1 minute to coat the steak.

To assemble the bowls, scoop tri-veggie rice into four bowls and top with the garlic Mongolian beef.

BAJA FISH TACO BOWL

Serves 4

There is nothing quite like the perfect fish taco. Living in Southern California, I have had my fair share of fish tacos and have found the key to a good one is a creamy slaw with a little kick to it and lots of lime squeezed on top. So enjoy your taco in a bowl, close your eyes and envision yourself sitting beachside!

Meat

1½ lb (680 g) cod, thawed if frozen

1½ tsp (4 g) chili powder

½ tsp cumin

½ tsp garlic powder

½ tsp onion powder

½ tsp smoked paprika

½ tsp salt

2 tbsp (30 ml) avocado or olive oil

Veggies

2 tbsp (30 ml) avocado or olive oil

8 cups (800 g) cauliflower rice

½ tsp chili powder

2 tsp (4 g) lime zest, divided

3 tbsp (45 ml) lime juice, divided

Salt and pepper

¼ cup (60 g) mayonnaise★

2 tbsp (2 g) chopped cilantro, divided, plus more for garnish

½ tsp smoked paprika

3 cups (210 g) coleslaw mix (or 1½ cups [105 g] each green and red cabbage)

Meat

Place the cod on a plate. In a small bowl, combine the chili powder, cumin, garlic powder, onion powder, smoked paprika and salt. Pour the spice mix over the cod and press it into both sides.

Put a large skillet over medium heat and pour the oil in the pan. Place the cod in the pan and cook for 2 minutes, then flip and cook for 3 minutes or until cooked through. Set it aside.

Veggies

In the same large skillet, add the oil and the cauliflower rice. Cook for 4 minutes, stirring occasionally. Add the chili powder, 1 teaspoon of lime zest and 2 tablespoons (30 ml) of lime juice, and stir to combine. Cook for 3 to 5 minutes, or until the cauliflower rice is cooked through. Season with salt and pepper to taste.

In medium bowl, combine the mayonnaise, 1 tablespoon (15 ml) of lime juice, 1 teaspoon of lime zest, cilantro and smoked paprika. Whisk until combined, then add the coleslaw mix and toss to coat. Season with salt and pepper to taste.

To assemble the bowls, divide the cauliflower rice among four bowls and top each with a slice of fish and cilantro-lime slaw. Garnish with additional cilantro.

★ Mayonnaise: When I use mayo in this book, I am always using an avocado oil–based mayonnaise with clean ingredients. There are a lot of mayonnaise options now, but the ingredients are so important here for it to be Paleo. My favorite brand is Primal Kitchen.

SESAME CHICKEN LETTUCE WRAP BOWL

Serves 4

Oh, lettuce wraps. I love them so much, I put them in a bowl so they could make the cut for this book because it's seriously unbelievable that these are Paleo. The key to these is finely chopping the chicken. Use a large knife or kitchen shears to get them to the perfect size, so all of the yummy sauce can coat each little bit.

Meat

2 tbsp (30 ml) sesame oil

1 lb (454 g) boneless, skinless chicken, finely chopped

¼ cup (60 ml) coconut aminos

1 tbsp (15 ml) rice wine vinegar

1 tbsp (15 ml) tahini

1 tbsp (15 ml) honey

1 tsp arrowroot powder

½ tsp garlic powder

½ tsp ground ginger

Salt and pepper

Veggies

1 (8-oz [226-g]) can water chestnuts, drained and finely chopped

2 scallions, chopped

Butter lettuce

Meat

Place a large skillet over medium heat. Pour the sesame oil in the pan. Once the oil is hot, add the chicken and spread it out evenly. Cook for 2 minutes, stir, then cook for another 2 minutes.

While the chicken cooks, make your sauce. Combine the coconut aminos, rice wine vinegar, tahini, honey, arrowroot powder, garlic powder and ginger. Pour the sauce over the chicken and continue to cook while stirring for 2 minutes until the chicken is cooked and the sauce is thickened. Season with salt and pepper to taste.

Veggies

Stir the water chestnuts and scallions into the chicken mixture. Line the bottom of your bowls with butter lettuce and scoop the chicken into the lettuce cups.

Prep Ahead: Make the meat up to 4 days ahead of time and store in the fridge.

CHICKEN EGG ROLL MEATBALL BOWL

Serves 4

When you are eating clean and doing your best not to order takeout, you can really start to crave the classics. My favorite part of a chicken egg roll is the dipping sauce anyways, so I made a bowl of yummy cabbage and veggies, topped it with some super flavorful chicken meatballs and then drizzled tons of sauce on top. When you take all of the best parts of a recipe and leave out the vegetable oil and refined flours, anything can become Paleo!

Meat

1 lb (454 g) ground chicken

2 tsp (2 g) grated fresh ginger

2 tsp (6 g) minced garlic

1 large egg

½ cup (74 g) almond flour

¼ cup (10 g) chopped scallions (white part)

1 tsp salt

¼ tsp pepper

Veggies

1 head of cabbage, thinly sliced

2 cups (220 g) shredded carrots

¾ cup (31 g) chopped scallions (green parts only)

2 tbsp (30 ml) sesame oil

Salt and pepper

Sauce

¼ cup (60 ml) coconut aminos

¼ cup (60 ml) rice vinegar

1 tbsp (15 ml) sesame oil

½ tsp ground ginger

½ tsp garlic powder

½ tsp onion powder

¼ tsp mustard powder

½ tsp arrowroot powder

Meat

Preheat the oven to 400°F (200°C, or gas mark 6). Line a baking sheet with foil. In a large bowl, combine the chicken, ginger, garlic, egg, almond flour, the white part of the scallions, salt and pepper. Once thoroughly combined, form into 16 meatballs and place them on the baking sheet. Bake for 20 minutes.

Veggies

Place a large skillet over medium heat. Add half of the cabbage, the carrots and the greens of the scallions. Pour the oil on top and mix together to lightly coat the veggies. Wilt for about 6 minutes, then add the rest of the cabbage and cook for 5 to 7 minutes until reduced by half. Season with salt and pepper.

Sauce

In a small bowl, combine the coconut aminos, rice vinegar, sesame oil, ginger, garlic powder, onion powder, mustard powder and arrowroot powder. Place a small skillet over medium heat and once warmed, pour in the sauce. Because the pan is hot, the mixture will boil when it hits the pan. Cook and whisk until the sauce has thickened and can coat the back of a spoon, about 3 to 5 minutes.

To assemble the bowls, divide the veggies into four bowls and top each with 4 meatballs and drizzle with the sauce.

Prep Ahead: Make the meatballs and chop the cabbage, carrots and scallions up to 4 days ahead of time and store them in the fridge separately. The sauce can be made up to 1 week ahead of time and kept in a jar in the fridge. Before putting the dish together, shake the sauce thoroughly so no arrowroot powder is left stuck at the bottom.

GYRO MEATBALL BOWL   Serves 4

My Lemon-Herb Tahini Sauce (page 37) is just too good to be used on only one recipe in this book! I had to have a gyro recipe in here because my hubby loves it so much. While ground lamb isn't usually on our weekly grocery list, this recipe is a fun and delicious way to mix up your weeknights and keep things clean!

Meat
½ white onion

1 lb (454 g) ground lamb

1 tbsp (1 g) dried marjoram

2 tsp (3 g) garlic powder

1 tsp oregano

¼ cup (37 g) almond flour

1 tsp salt

¼ tsp pepper

Veggies
2 tbsp (30 ml) avocado or olive oil, divided

6 cups (600 g) cauliflower rice

1 tsp garlic powder

2 tbsp (30 ml) lemon juice, divided

Salt

2 cups (298 g) chopped cherry tomatoes

1 cup (104 g) chopped cucumber

½ cup (80 g) chopped red onion

1 tbsp (4 g) chopped fresh parsley

Pepper

For Serving
Lemon-Herb Tahini Sauce (page 37)

Meat
Preheat the oven to 350°F (175°C, or gas mark 4). Oil an 8 x 8–inch (20 x 20–cm) glass baking dish.

Mince the onion with a microplane or small grater onto paper towels. Squeeze the liquid out of the onion, then add it to a food processor. Add the lamb, marjoram, garlic powder, oregano, almond flour, salt and pepper and blend for about 1 minute, until combined and smooth. Form into 16 meatballs and place them in the oiled glass dish. Bake for 15 minutes. Turn your oven to broil on high, wait 5 minutes and return the meatballs to the oven for 1 minute, or until lightly browned.

Veggies
Place a large skillet over medium heat and pour 1 tablespoon (15 ml) of oil in the pan. Add the cauliflower rice and cook for 5 minutes, stirring occasionally. Add the garlic powder and 1 tablespoon (15 ml) of lemon juice and continue to cook for 2 to 3 minutes, or until tender. Season with salt to taste.

In a medium bowl, combine the cherry tomatoes, cucumber, onion, parsley, 1 tablespoon (15 ml) of lemon juice and 1 tablespoon (15 ml) of oil. Season with salt and pepper to taste.

To assemble the bowls, scoop the cauliflower rice into each bowl and top with the cherry tomato salad, meatballs and a drizzle of the tahini sauce.

Prep Ahead: Make the meatballs up to 4 days ahead of time and store them in the fridge. The sauce can be made up to 2 weeks ahead of time and stored in the fridge. Tahini seizes up in the fridge so when you are ready to serve, thin the sauce out slightly by adding 1 tablespoon (15 ml) of water at a time until your desired consistency is achieved.

SWEET MANDARIN CHICKEN WITH TRI-VEGGIE RICE

Back in college we had a Panda Express on campus. I used to go crazy there and I loved their mandarin chicken, especially because I thought I was being healthy by eating it. It wasn't fried right?! Little did I know the sauce was filled with processed soy and corn syrup and probably not the best bet. So, I created a cleaned-up version that I might just love even more!

Meat

1 lb (454 g) chicken thighs

2 tbsp (30 ml) avocado or olive oil

½ tsp salt

2 tbsp (25 g) coconut sugar

¼ cup (60 ml) coconut aminos

1 tsp lemon juice

½ tsp garlic powder

¼ tsp ground ginger

⅓ cup (80 ml) water

1 tsp arrowroot powder plus 1 tbsp (15 ml) water

Veggies

1 head of cauliflower, chopped

1 head of broccoli, chopped

1 large sweet potato, peeled and chopped

2 tbsp (30 ml) avocado or olive oil

2 tbsp (30 ml) coconut aminos

Salt and pepper

Meat

In a medium bowl, combine the chicken thighs, oil and salt. Place a large skillet over medium heat and add the chicken thighs. Cook for 3 to 4 minutes per side, or until the chicken is cooked through, then set it aside.

In a small bowl, combine the coconut sugar, coconut aminos, lemon juice, garlic powder, ginger and water, then add it to the pan that the chicken was cooked in, keeping it over medium heat. Bring to a simmer, then add the arrowroot mixture and whisk vigorously to thicken. Chop the chicken and add it to the pan to coat with the sauce. Simmer on the lowest heat possible while you cook the veggie rice.

Veggies

Place the shredder attachment on a food processor and put the cauliflower, broccoli and sweet potato through the top part of the attachment to turn it into "rice." If you don't have a food processor you can also manually grate the veggies with a cheese grater.

Place a large skillet over medium heat and pour the oil in the pan. Add the veggie rice and stir. Cook for 5 minutes then add the coconut aminos and continue to cook, covered, for 3 to 5 minutes until the sweet potato pieces are tender. Season with salt and pepper to taste.

To assemble the bowls, divide the veggie rice among four bowls and top each with mandarin chicken.

Prep Ahead: Make the entire protein portion up to 4 days ahead of time, store it in the fridge and reheat it on the stovetop. Make the cauliflower, broccoli and sweet potato into rice in your food processor and store it in your fridge but wait to cook it until it's time to eat.

CHICKEN POKE BOWL

Serves 4

I love a poke bowl as much as the next gal, but something about buying and eating raw fish at home is a little scary. So, to get the same flavors and toppings with none of the scaries, I made a chicken version! Thanks to coconut aminos, we have a soy sauce alternative that completes this meal. It's everything you want in a poke stop without being 35 percent sure you're going to poison yourself.

Meat

1 tbsp (15 ml) avocado or olive oil

1 lb (454 g) boneless, skinless chicken breasts

Salt and pepper

Veggies

1 tbsp (15 ml) avocado or olive oil

4 cups (400 g) cauliflower rice

3 tbsp (45 ml) coconut aminos★

1 tsp garlic powder

½ tsp ground ginger

Salt and pepper

¼ cup (28 g) shredded carrots

¼ cup (26 g) chopped cucumber

1 medium avocado, pitted, peeled and chopped

1 tbsp (8 g) toasted sesame seeds

4 lime wedges

Meat

Place a large skillet over medium heat and let it warm up. Pour the oil in the pan. Sprinkle the chicken breasts with salt and pepper on both sides, then add them to the pan. Cook the chicken for 3 minutes per side, or until cooked through. Set the chicken aside to cool slightly, then chop it into cubes.

Veggies

Add the oil into the same pan over medium heat, then add the cauliflower rice. Cook the cauliflower rice for 3 minutes, stirring occasionally, then add the coconut aminos, garlic powder and ginger. Stir to combine and cook for 2 to 3 minutes, or until the cauliflower rice is cooked and tender. Season to taste with salt and pepper.

To assemble the bowls, divide the cauliflower rice among four bowls and top each with chicken, carrots, cucumber, avocado and some toasted sesame seeds. Serve with a lime wedge.

★ Coconut Aminos: A soy sauce replacement in Paleo cooking. Salty and slightly sweet, it is a staple in our house at all times. It is made from the sap of coconut palms and has 73 percent less sodium than soy sauce.

Prep Ahead: Cook the chicken and cauliflower rice up to 4 days ahead of time, and store them separately in the fridge. Add the carrots, cucumber, avocado, sesame seeds and lime when it's time to eat.

CHICKEN ENCHILADA BOWL

Serves 4

Everyone has a go-to order at certain restaurants, right? If we go get Mexican food, chances are I am ordering enchiladas, unless we are by the water, then it's fish tacos. I love an enchilada that is coated in sauce and this bowl hits that mark! The more sauce the better, because it drips down to coat the cauliflower rice and leaves you wanting more.

Meat

1 lb (454 g) boneless chicken thighs

½ tsp salt

¼ tsp pepper

Sauce

2 tbsp (30 ml) avocado or olive oil

2 tbsp (15 g) chili powder

1 (8-oz [227-g]) can tomato sauce

¼ cup (60 ml) chicken broth

2 tsp (3 g) ground cumin

1 tbsp (9 g) minced garlic

½ tsp onion powder

¼ tsp salt

Veggies

3 tbsp (45 ml) avocado or olive oil, divided

2 medium bell peppers, chopped

8 cups (800 g) cauliflower rice

2 tbsp (32 g) tomato paste

2 tbsp (30 ml) chicken broth

Salt and pepper

Meat

Preheat the oven to 350°F (175°C, or gas mark 4). Line a baking sheet with parchment paper and place the chicken thighs on the baking sheet. Sprinkle the chicken with salt and pepper. Bake for 18 minutes, then remove it from the oven and shred the chicken.

Sauce

In a blender, combine the oil, chili powder, tomato sauce, broth, cumin, garlic, onion powder and salt. Place the chicken in a bowl, pour on the sauce and toss to coat.

Veggies

Place a large skillet over medium heat and pour in 2 tablespoons (30 ml) of oil and add the bell peppers. Cook, stirring occasionally, for 5 minutes until tender. Remove and set it aside.

Add 1 tablespoon (15 ml) of oil to the same pan, followed by the cauliflower rice and cook, stirring occasionally, for 3 minutes. Add the tomato paste and broth and stir to combine. Season with salt and pepper to taste. Cook for 2 to 3 minutes, or until tender.

To assemble the bowls, scoop the cauliflower rice evenly into four bowls and top with the bell peppers and enchilada chicken.

Prep Ahead: Cook the chicken, make the sauce and combine the two up to 4 days ahead of time and store in the fridge.

Vivacious & Veggie-Packed

I haven't always liked veggies . . . shocker, right? Honestly, who has though?! Most of us don't realize the potential of veggies until we are well into adulthood, but when you do, it's glorious! A whole new world opens up once you learn how to cook them properly, what spices to put on them and how to pair them with protein. Veggies can finally become an exciting part of a meal instead of the sad sidekick!

In this chapter, you will find some vegetarian dishes that will shock you with flavor. Some bowls, such as the Asian Beef Burrito Bowl with Ginger-Avocado Crema (page 81), highlight a base of incredible veggie-cauliflower rice mixtures. For a warm salad to keep you happy and feeling strong, try my Roasted Root Veggie Salad with Sweet Mustard Dressing (page 73). I love to think of veggie-packed meals as a real food multivitamin; each different veggie has so many great nutrients. It is pretty incredible to thoroughly enjoy something that will help you live a long and healthy life!

ROASTED ROOT VEGGIE SALAD WITH SWEET MUSTARD DRESSING

Serves 4

I think I need to put a warning with this recipe: If you make this salad, you will want to drink the dressing. But this is a reminder that it is meant to coat the salad and not be a thick and delicious beverage. Don't put a straw in it—pour it on these roasted veggies, devour them and be utterly shocked that this creamy goodness is Paleo.

Veggies

1 onion, chopped

2 large sweet potatoes, peeled and cubed

1 bulb of fennel, chopped

3 cups (384 g) chopped carrots

2 beets, peeled and chopped

2 tsp (6 g) minced garlic

2 tbsp (30 ml) avocado or olive oil

1 tsp dried oregano

1 tsp ground fennel

1 tsp salt

½ tsp pepper

8 cups (160 g) arugula

Dressing

¼ cup (59 g) mayonnaise★

2 tbsp (30 ml) Dijon mustard

2 tsp (10 ml) whole-grain mustard

2 tbsp (30 ml) maple syrup

1 tbsp (15 ml) apple cider vinegar

Salt and pepper

Veggies

Preheat the oven to 400°F (200°C, or gas mark 6). In a large bowl, combine the onion, sweet potatoes, fennel bulb, carrots, beets, garlic, oil, oregano, ground fennel, salt and pepper. Toss to coat the veggies.

Pour the veggies onto two separate foil-lined baking sheets and spread them into an even layer. Roast for 45 minutes, stirring them halfway through.

Dressing

In a small bowl, combine the mayonnaise, Dijon mustard, whole-grain mustard, maple syrup and apple cider vinegar. Season with salt and pepper to taste.

To build the salads, place 2 cups (40 g) of arugula in the bottom of each bowl, and top with veggies and a drizzle of the dressing.

★: Mayonnaise: When I use mayo in this book, I am always using an avocado oil–based mayonnaise with clean ingredients. There are a lot of mayonnaise options now, but the ingredients are so important here for it to be Paleo. My favorite brand is Primal Kitchen.

Prep Ahead: All of the veggies except for the arugula can be roasted up to 4 days ahead of time and kept in the fridge, then reheated on the stovetop. The dressing can be made up to 2 weeks ahead of time and stored in the fridge.

HONEY-LIME-GINGER MEATBALL BOWL   Serves 4

I am always looking for a little bit of a zing in a recipe, which usually means adding some kind of acid. In this recipe we get a double zing from lime and ginger, then it all comes together with a sweet honey sauce which helps moisten the lean meatballs. This bowl is a perfect balance of nutrients and flavor!

Meat
½ lb (226 g) ground pork
½ lb (226 g) ground turkey
1 large egg
¼ cup (37 g) almond flour
Zest of 1 lime
1 tsp ground ginger
½ tsp garlic powder
1 tsp salt

Sauce
½ cup (120 ml) coconut aminos
½ cup (120 ml) lime juice
2 tbsp (30 ml) honey
1 tsp ground ginger
1 tsp arrowroot powder plus 1 tbsp (15 ml) water

Veggies
1 head of cauliflower, chopped
1 head of broccoli, chopped
1 large (130 g) sweet potato, peeled and chopped
2 tbsp (30 ml) avocado or olive oil
2 tbsp (30 ml) coconut aminos
Salt and pepper

Meat
Preheat the oven to 350°F (175°C, or gas mark 4) and line a baking sheet with foil.

In a bowl combine the pork, turkey, egg, almond flour, lime zest, ginger, garlic powder and salt. Mix with your hands until well combined.

Form into 16 meatballs and place them on the foil-lined baking sheet. Bake meatballs for 18 minutes.

Sauce
While the meatballs cook, combine the coconut aminos, lime juice, honey and ginger in a bowl. Whisk to combine.

Pour the sauce in a skillet over medium heat and whisk until it boils. Add the arrowroot mixture and whisk vigorously to combine. The sauce should thicken quickly so take it off the heat as soon as it has thickened, about 15 to 30 seconds.

Veggies
Place the shredder attachment on a food processor and put the cauliflower, broccoli and sweet potato through to turn it into "rice." If you don't have a food processor you can also manually grate the veggies with a cheese grater.

Place a large skillet over medium heat and pour the oil in the pan. Add the veggie rice and stir. Cook for 5 minutes then add the coconut aminos. Continue to cook, covered, for 3 to 5 minutes, or until the sweet potato pieces are tender. Season with salt and pepper to taste.

To make the bowls, divide the veggie rice among four bowls, add 4 meatballs to each bowl and top with your desired amount of sauce.

Prep Ahead: Make the meatballs and chop the veggies into rice up to 4 days ahead of time and store separately in the fridge.

SUN-DRIED TOMATO PESTO ZUCCHINI PASTA SALAD

If you need a knockout dish to bring to a summer party, this is it! I love using raw zucchini in dishes like this because it holds up in the fridge for a few days, has the perfect amount of bite to it and has the fiber and protein to make it a great base for a meal. Also, sun-dried tomatoes are my love language, so this salad is absolutely the way to my heart!

Sauce

1 (6-oz [170-g]) jar sun-dried tomatoes in avocado or olive oil

1 tsp minced garlic

1 cup (24 g) basil

¼ cup (34 g) pine nuts

¼ cup (27 g) nutritional yeast

1 tbsp (15 ml) lemon juice

Salt and pepper

Veggies

6 medium zucchinis, peeled

1 cup (149 g) chopped cherry tomatoes

¼ cup (27 g) chopped Kalamata olives

Sauce

In a food processor, pour in the sun-dried tomatoes including the oil with the garlic, basil, pine nuts, nutritional yeast and lemon juice. Blend on high until the sun-dried tomatoes have broken down. Season to taste with salt and pepper.

Veggies

Chop the ends off of the zucchini, then chop them in half. Make a slice lengthwise, halfway through the zucchini. Place the zucchini in a spiralizer on blade C if using an Inspiralizer.★ Spiralize and repeat with the remaining zucchini.

Place the zucchini pasta into a large bowl with cherry tomatoes and olives. Pour the sauce over the top and toss to combine.

✳   The Inspiralizer is a brand of spiralizer that I love and recommend!

Prep Ahead: Make this whole dish up to 4 days ahead of time and store in the fridge. Eat it cold!

CITRUS-MARINATED CARNE ASADA ON CILANTRO-LIME CAULIFLOWER RICE

Serves 4

I'm about to hit you with a pro-tip: Always have bottled lime and lemon juice on hand. You can buy it organic, and it lasts for a long time. And it is so perfect to add to sauces, marinades and, of course, cocktails. I love a citrus marinade because it makes the meat taste delicious and also helps break it down and make it tender!

Meat

1½ lb (680 g) carne asada★
¼ cup (60 ml) lime juice
¼ cup (60 ml) orange juice
1 tsp salt
¼ tsp paprika
½ tsp garlic powder
¼ cup (60 ml) avocado or olive oil, divided

Veggies

1 tbsp (15 ml) avocado or olive oil
8 cups (800 g) cauliflower rice
2 tbsp (2 g) chopped cilantro
¼ cup (60 ml) lime juice
1 tsp garlic powder
Salt
1 cup (149 g) chopped cherry tomatoes
1 avocado, pitted, peeled and sliced

Meat

In a large plastic bag or glass dish, combine the carne asada, lime juice, orange juice, salt, paprika, garlic powder and 2 tablespoons (30 ml) of oil. Close the bag almost completely, then suck out the remaining air in the bag to vacuum seal it. If you are short on time, let it sit out on the counter for at least 30 minutes or in the fridge for up to 12 hours.

Place a large skillet over medium heat and pour 2 tablespoons (30 ml) of oil in the pan. Place the carne asada in the pan and cook for 3 to 4 minutes per side. When the meat is cooked, set it aside and let sit for 10 minutes before slicing into strips.

Veggies

Place a large skillet over medium heat and pour the oil in the pan. Add the cauliflower rice and cook, stirring occasionally, for 5 minutes. Add the cilantro, lime juice and garlic powder and toss to coat. Cook for 2 to 4 minutes, or until the rice is tender. Season with salt to taste.

To assemble the bowls, divide the cauliflower rice among four bowls and top each with the carne asada, cherry tomatoes and avocado.

★ Sometimes labeled "sliced sirloin flap meat."

Prep Ahead: Marinate the carne asada up to 2 days before cooking.

ASIAN BEEF BURRITO BOWL WITH GINGER-AVOCADO CREMA
Serves 4

There are many recipes in this book that are already staples in our house, but this one is definitely near the top of the list. A simple sauce poured over ground beef and cauliflower rice can somehow transform it into an irresistible meal that the whole family will devour. This recipe is made for four, but I'm pretty sure my husband ate two-thirds of it right after I made it—you've been warned!

Meat
1 tbsp (15 ml) avocado or olive oil
1 tsp minced garlic
1 lb (454 g) ground beef
⅓ cup (80 ml) coconut aminos
2 tbsp (30 ml) honey
1 tbsp (15 ml) sesame oil
1 tsp arrowroot powder
½ tsp ground ginger
½ tsp garlic powder
Salt and pepper

Veggies
2 tbsp (30 ml) sesame oil
6 cups (600 g) cauliflower rice
1½ cups (165 g) shredded carrots
1 cup (110 g) chopped green beans
2 tbsp (30 ml) coconut aminos
1 tsp ground ginger
1 tsp garlic powder
Salt and pepper

Sauce
1 avocado, pitted and peeled
¼ cup (60 ml) coconut milk
2 tbsp (30 ml) rice wine vinegar
1 tbsp (15 ml) lemon juice
½ tsp grated fresh ginger
Salt

Meat
Place a large skillet over medium heat. Pour the oil in the pan then add the garlic. Cook the garlic for 1 minute, then add the beef. Cook the beef, while breaking it up with a wooden spoon, for about 5 minutes until cooked through.

While the beef is cooking, combine the coconut aminos, honey, sesame oil, arrowroot powder, ginger and garlic powder in a small bowl. Once the beef is cooked, pour the mixture over it and stir quickly to combine. Cook for 1 minute, then remove it from the heat and season to taste with salt and pepper.

Veggies
Place a separate large skillet over medium heat and pour the sesame oil in the pan. Add the cauliflower rice, carrots and green beans to the pan. Stir to combine. Cook the veggies for 5 to 7 minutes, or until the cauliflower rice is soft. Add the coconut aminos, ginger and garlic powder, and stir to coat. Season to taste with salt and pepper.

Sauce
In a blender, combine the avocado, coconut milk, rice wine vinegar, lemon juice and ginger. Blend on high until smooth and season with salt to taste.

To assemble the bowls, divide the veggie rice between four bowls, top each with Asian beef and drizzle on the ginger-avocado crema.

Prep Ahead: The Asian beef can be made up to 4 days ahead of time and stored in the fridge.

ALOHA BITES BOWL

Serves 4

This bowl all started with this epic Paleo Hawaiian BBQ sauce. It's one of those sauces you make and think, "I don't even care what you put it on, just get it on my plate!" So, you can whip it up quickly, toss it over chicken and put that on some simple coconut cauliflower rice with pineapple, and ALOHA flavor. This is the type of meal that you won't believe is mostly vegetables!

Hawaiian BBQ Sauce

1 (15-oz [425-g]) can tomato sauce

¼ cup (60 ml) apple cider vinegar

¼ cup (60 ml) pineapple juice

1 (8-oz [226-g]) can crushed pineapple, drained

¼ cup (60 ml) molasses

2 tbsp (25 g) coconut sugar

¼ cup (66 g) tomato paste

2 tbsp (30 ml) coconut aminos

¼ tsp ground mustard seed

½ tsp onion powder

¼ tsp ground ginger

½ tsp garlic powder

½ tsp pepper

½ tsp salt

Meat

1 lb (454 g) boneless, skinless chicken breasts

2 tbsp (30 ml) avocado or olive oil

Veggies

2 tbsp (30 ml) avocado or olive oil

1 cup (160 g) chopped red onion

2 medium bell peppers, chopped

8 cups (800 g) cauliflower rice

½ cup (120 ml) full-fat coconut milk

1 tsp ground ginger

½ tsp garlic powder

Salt

2 cups (330 g) chopped pineapple

Chopped cilantro

Sauce

Pour the tomato sauce, apple cider vinegar, pineapple juice, pineapple, molasses, coconut sugar, tomato paste, coconut aminos, mustard seed, onion powder, ginger, garlic powder, pepper and salt in a blender. Blend on high until combined, about 20 to 30 seconds. Set it aside.

Meat

Chop up the chicken into bite-size pieces and place them in a bowl. Add 1 cup (240 ml) of the sauce to the chicken and let it marinate for 30 to 60 minutes.

Once the chicken has marinated, place a large skillet over medium-high heat. When the pan is warm, pour the oil in the pan and let it heat up. Add the chicken and spread it into an even layer. Let it sit and cook on one side for 3 minutes. Flip and cook it on the other side for 3 minutes until cooked through. Remove from the pan.

Veggies

Place another large skillet over medium heat and pour the oil in the pan. Add the onion and bell peppers and cook, stirring occasionally, for 3 minutes. Add the cauliflower rice and cook for 3 minutes. Add the coconut milk, ginger and garlic powder to the veggies and stir. Continue to cook for 3 to 4 minutes, or until the cauliflower rice is tender and season with salt to taste.

To assemble the bowls, scoop the coconut cauliflower rice into each bowl and top each of them with chicken, pineapple and cilantro. Drizzle with extra Hawaiian BBQ sauce, if desired.

Prep Ahead: Make the BBQ sauce up to 2 weeks in advance and cook the chicken up to 4 days in advance. Store both in the fridge.

ROASTED CURRY VEGETABLE POWER BOWL

This sauce. This sauce should be in a hall of fame somewhere. Just a picture of me, holding a bowl of it and weeping because it's so delicious, behind glass where people can come and buy this book. These are the things I think about because, if you haven't caught on, I love food. This sauce is so good that all you have to do is roast some veggies, drizzle this on and call it a meal!

Veggies

2 cups (200 g) chopped cauliflower

2 cups (256 g) chopped carrots

1 medium sweet potato, peeled and chopped

2 cups (220 g) chopped green beans

2 tbsp (30 ml) avocado or olive oil

1 tsp curry powder

½ tsp ground ginger

½ tsp garlic powder

1 tsp salt

½ tsp pepper

1 (16-oz [454-g]) bag arugula

Sauce

¼ cup (56 g) cashew butter

1 tsp curry powder

½ cup (120 ml) coconut milk

½ tsp garlic powder

¼ tsp ground ginger

Salt and pepper

Veggies

Preheat the oven to 425°F (220°C, or gas mark 7). Line two baking sheets with parchment paper and place the cauliflower, carrots, sweet potato and green beans on one of the pans. Add the oil and toss to coat the veggies. Sprinkle on curry powder, ginger, garlic powder, salt and pepper. Toss to coat. Divide between the two pans into one even layer.

Roast the veggies for 30 to 35 minutes, stirring them halfway, until the sweet potatoes are slightly crispy.

Sauce

In a small bowl, combine the cashew butter, curry powder, coconut milk, garlic powder and ginger. Whisk to combine. Season with salt and pepper to taste.

To assemble the bowls, divide the arugula among four bowls and top each with roasted veggies. Drizzle the sauce over each bowl.

Prep Ahead: The veggies—excluding the arugula—can be roasted up to 3 days ahead of time and stored in the fridge. The sauce can be made up to 1 week ahead of time and stored in the fridge.

WARM GINGER-SCALLION PORK & KALE SALAD Serves 4

Oh, the wonderful world of a warm salad. Kale is great but it definitely needs a little TLC to really shine, so serving it warm with lots of flavor is a total Paleo win. Treat your kale like you treat an old friend, with a nice warm hug and a bit of sass.

Meat

1 tbsp (15 ml) avocado or olive oil

1 lb (454 g) ground pork

1 tsp ground ginger

½ tsp garlic powder

1 tbsp (15 ml) coconut aminos

1 tsp salt

⅓ cup (33 g) chopped scallions

Dressing

2 tbsp (30 ml) avocado or olive oil

1 tbsp (15 ml) rice vinegar

1 tbsp (15 ml) coconut aminos★

1 tbsp (15 ml) honey

½ tsp grated fresh ginger

Veggies

2 bunches of kale, de-stemmed and chopped

1 cup (110 g) shredded carrots

Toasted sesame seeds

Meat

Place a large skillet over medium heat. Once the pan is warm, pour in the oil. Add the pork and break it up with a wooden spoon or spatula as it cooks. After about 2 minutes of cooking, add the ginger, garlic powder, coconut aminos and salt. Stir in the spices and continue to cook for 2 to 3 minutes, or until all the pink is gone. Add the scallions and stir to combine, then set the pork aside.

Dressing

In a small bowl, whisk together the oil, rice vinegar, coconut aminos, honey and ginger. Place a large skillet over medium heat and add the dressing to the pan.

Veggies

Add the kale to the dressing in the pan and toss with tongs to coat the kale. Cover the skillet and let it cook for 2 minutes to wilt the kale slightly, stirring occasionally. Add the carrots and toss, then cook for 30 seconds.

To assemble the bowls, divide the dressed kale and carrots among four bowls, top each bowl with pork and garnish with toasted sesame seeds.

★ Coconut Aminos: A soy sauce replacement in Paleo cooking. Salty and slightly sweet, it is a staple in our house at all times. It is made from the sap of coconut palms and has 73 percent less sodium than soy sauce.

Prep Ahead: Make the protein and dressing up to 5 days ahead of time and store them separately in the fridge. Reheat each on the stovetop and continue with the recipe.

BRUSSELS SPROUT & DATE CHOPPED SALAD Serves 4

There is a café near my house that has a Brussels sprout salad with dates and Parmesan that I get every time I go. So, I made a version for you that is dairy-free but not lacking any flavor! Adding nutritional yeast to the dressing gives it a little cheesy flavor and the chopped dates add a fabulous texture and sweetness that is to die for.

Veggies

2 lb (907 g) Brussels sprouts

4 cups (268 g) thinly sliced kale

8 Medjool dates, pitted

¼ cup (31 g) shelled pistachios, chopped

Dressing

¼ cup (60 ml) olive oil

¼ cup (60 ml) balsamic vinegar

1 tbsp (10 g) minced shallots

1 tbsp (15 ml) Dijon mustard

1 tbsp (15 ml) honey

2 tbsp (5 g) nutritional yeast

Salt and pepper

Veggies

Slice the ends off of each Brussels sprout, then thinly slice them with a knife or in the slicing attachment of your food processor. In a large bowl, combine the Brussels sprouts, kale, dates and pistachios.

Dressing

In a blender, combine the oil, balsamic vinegar, shallots, Dijon mustard, honey and nutritional yeast. Blend on high for 30 seconds to combine, then season with salt and pepper.

Pour the dressing over the salad and massage the dressing into the greens with your hands. Divide among four bowls.

Prep Ahead: The Brussels sprouts and kale can be chopped up to 4 days ahead of time and stored in the fridge. The dressing can be made up to 1 week ahead of time and stored in the fridge.

Vivacious & Veggie-Packed 89

FENNEL & GARLIC TURKEY MEATBALLS ON ZOODLES

A couple of years ago my hubby and I somehow discovered that fennel is incredible. I think we made a recipe that called for it, and once we started using it, we put it in everything. No breakfast sausage is complete without it, and with it, these turkey meatballs are next level!

Meat

1 lb (454 g) ground turkey

1 large egg

¼ cup (37 g) almond flour

½ tsp minced garlic

1 tsp ground fennel

1 tsp garlic powder

1 tsp salt

½ tsp pepper

Veggies

2 cups (480 ml) marinara sauce, divided

6 medium zucchinis

1 tbsp (15 ml) avocado or olive oil

2 cups (298 g) chopped cherry tomatoes

Salt and pepper

Meat

Preheat the oven to 400°F (200°C, or gas mark 6) and line a baking sheet with parchment paper. In a medium bowl, combine the turkey, egg, almond flour, garlic, fennel, garlic powder, salt and pepper. Stir to combine evenly. Form into 16 meatballs and place them on the baking sheet. Bake for 16 minutes or until cooked through.

Veggies

In a small pot, warm the marinara sauce. Slice off the ends of each zucchini. Use a spiralizer to cut the zucchini into zoodles (zucchini noodles). Place a large skillet over medium heat and pour the oil in the pan. Add the zoodles and cherry tomatoes. Cook, tossing occasionally, for 5 minutes until the zoodles are tender but not soggy. Add 1 cup (240 ml) of marinara sauce and toss to coat. Season with salt and pepper to taste.

To assemble the bowls, scoop zoodles into each bowl and top with 4 meatballs. Drizzle each bowl with ¼ cup (60 ml) of warmed marinara sauce.

Prep Ahead: Make the meatballs up to 4 days ahead of time and store them in the fridge. The meatballs are also freezer friendly! Cook the meatballs according to the recipe instructions, let them cool and freeze them in an airtight container. To reheat, place the meatballs in a glass dish and bake covered at 350°F (175°C) for 30 minutes.

Wake Up to WOW

The best part of waking up is . . . usually a large Americano for me. Then, I get a cuddle from my kiddo, and then a delicious and healthy breakfast. Throughout my life I have ventured into every breakfast vortex you can think of looking for the perfect way to start my morning. There was the low-fat yogurt stage—cringe—and then the instant oatmeal packet phase and then I moved on to the protein bar stage. In the end, all these left me feeling hangry two hours later. I now know the only way to start the morning is with a nourishing bowl of Paleo goodness.

This chapter brings you my favorite breakfasts that are easy to make each morning. They are also wonderful when meal prepping for the week. They are full of nutrients, protein and fat to help you feel fuller for longer—and that keeps you away from those sweets at the office or coffee shop! From savory to sweet, I cover all the bases so you can start your morning happy, healthy and ready for anything the day throws at you!

SWEET POTATO, KALE & CHICKEN SAUSAGE BOWL

Serves 4

This is my favorite go-to breakfast. Sweet potatoes, greens and homemade chicken sausage is just about the perfect way to start your day. The chicken gives you that boost of protein to keep you full, the sweet potatoes have carbs for fast-acting energy and the kale has incredible micronutrients and vitamins to keep your body working the way it should! I love making a double batch of these chicken sausages and freezing them for later!

Meat

2 tbsp (30 ml) avocado or olive oil, divided

½ cup (80 g) finely chopped yellow onion

1 lb (454 g) ground chicken

1 tsp ground sage

½ tsp ground fennel

¼ tsp cinnamon

1 tsp salt

Veggies

1 tbsp (15 ml) avocado or olive oil

2 large sweet potatoes, peeled and cubed

1 bunch of kale, de-stemmed and chopped

1 tsp garlic powder

Salt and pepper

1 medium avocado, pitted, peeled and diced

Meat

Place a large skillet over medium heat. Once the pan is warm, pour in 1 tablespoon (15 ml) of the oil and add the onion. Cook, stirring occasionally, for 5 minutes until slightly browned. Set it aside.

In a medium bowl, add the chicken, sage, fennel, cinnamon, salt and the cooked onions. Mix with your hands or a wooden spoon to evenly combine.

Scoop the chicken into ¼-cup (60-ml)-sized balls and flatten them into 12 patties. In the same large skillet over medium heat, pour in 1 tablespoon (15 ml) of oil. Place 4 to 5 patties in the pan at a time so they aren't crowded. Cook for 2½ to 3 minutes per side, or until they are browned and cooked through.

Veggies

Place another large skillet over medium heat. Once the pan is warm, pour in the oil. Add the sweet potatoes and let them cook for 1 minute before stirring. Stir the sweet potatoes and continue cooking, stirring every 30 seconds, for about 5 to 7 minutes until they are fork tender.

Add the kale and garlic powder to the sweet potatoes. Stir and cover to let the kale wilt for about 30 seconds. Remove the lid and season to taste with salt and pepper.

To make the bowls, divide the sweet potato–kale mixture among four bowls and top each bowl with three chicken sausages and one-quarter of the avocado.

Prep Ahead: Make the chicken sausages up to 5 days ahead and store them in the fridge, or make them and freeze them in a single layer until frozen, then transfer them to an airtight container and keep them in the freezer for up to 3 months.

GARLIC-BACON-KALE BOWL

Serves 4

If kale could marry anyone, I know it would be bacon. They are a match made in heaven and balance each other out like soul mates should. Where kale lacks flavor, bacon comes in to help out. And where bacon lacks micronutrients, kale takes the reins and makes up for that! Throw that all in a bowl with an egg and you are set for a good day.

Protein
12 slices of bacon

4 eggs

Veggies
2 bunches of kale, de-stemmed and chopped

2 tsp (3 g) garlic powder

Salt and pepper

Protein
Place a large skillet over medium heat and cook the bacon until crispy, about 5 minutes per side. Remove and set it aside.

Once the bacon is cooked, leave the grease in the pan and fry the eggs until they are cooked to your liking. Chop the bacon and set both aside.

Veggies
To the remaining bacon grease, over medium heat, add the kale and cover, stirring every 20 to 30 seconds, until reduced by half, about 2 minutes. Add the garlic powder, and season with salt and pepper to taste.

Divide the kale into four bowls, then add 3 pieces of bacon and 1 egg to each.

SPICED FAJITA HASH BOWL

Serves 4

Fajitas are one of my favorite meals, so why not have them for breakfast? These are usually served with tortillas and cheese, but the most flavor comes from the meat and veggies, so that is our focus in this dish! This simple Paleo and egg-free option has all that delicious fajita flavor and will fuel your morning perfectly.

Meat

1 tbsp (15 ml) avocado or olive oil

1 lb (454 g) boneless, skinless chicken breasts

Salt and pepper

Veggies

2 tbsp (30 ml) avocado or olive oil

1 medium green bell pepper, chopped

1 medium red bell pepper, chopped

1 medium yellow onion, chopped

3 medium russet potatoes, peeled and chopped

1 tsp chili powder

½ tsp cumin

½ tsp garlic powder

½ tsp paprika

1 tsp salt, plus more to taste

¼ tsp pepper, plus more to taste

1 tsp arrowroot powder★

¼ cup (60 ml) chicken broth

2 avocados, pitted, peeled and sliced

Meat

Place a large skillet over medium heat. Once the pan is warm, pour in the oil. Sprinkle both sides of the chicken breasts with salt and pepper, then add them to the pan. Cook the chicken for 4 minutes per side, or until cooked through. Remove it and let it rest for 5 minutes.

Veggies

Into that same pan, pour the oil, then add the bell peppers and onion. Cook them for about 2 minutes, then add the potatoes. Stir everything to coat the veggies with oil, and cook for 3 minutes without stirring.

Stir the veggies. Cook, stirring occasionally, for 7 to 8 minutes until the potatoes are almost fork tender. Chop the chicken and add it to the pan.

In a small bowl, mix the chili powder, cumin, garlic powder, paprika, salt, pepper and arrowroot powder. Add the broth to the spice mixture and whisk to combine. Pour the spice blend into the pan and stir quickly to coat everything. Cover the pan and cook for 3 to 4 minutes. Season to taste with salt and pepper.

Divide the hash between four bowls and top each with sliced avocado.

★ Arrowroot Powder: A starch that is very versatile in Paleo cooking and baking. It is made from the root of a tropical plant called *Maranta arundinacea* and is essentially a cornstarch replacement. You may find it labeled "arrowroot flour" or "arrowroot starch," but they are all the same!

Prep Ahead: Make the whole dish, excluding the avocado, up to 5 days ahead of time. Store the bowls in the fridge and reheat them on the stovetop.

MICROWAVE FRITTATA BOWL   Serves 4

Sometimes you need an ultra-quick breakfast where you don't dirty a big pan. If you can pre-chop the veggies ahead of time, this meal comes together in less than five minutes, which is a huge win when it comes to Paleo breakfasts! The best part is that you can bring the prepped ingredients to work and make a gourmet meal right in the office kitchen.

Veggies
1 bell pepper, chopped
½ onion, chopped
2 cups (140 g) chopped white mushroom
1 cup (30 g) chopped spinach

Protein
12 eggs
Pinch of salt and pepper
Pinch of garlic powder
8 slices prosciutto, chopped

Veggies
Take four microwave-safe bowls and divide the bell pepper, onion, mushroom and spinach among them—about 1 cup (105 g) each. Add 1 teaspoon of water to the bowl and stir to combine. Microwave one bowl at a time for 45 seconds each to soften the veggies.

Protein
Add 3 eggs to each bowl with a pinch each of salt, pepper and garlic powder. Stir together with a fork. Microwave each bowl separately for 1½ minutes. Stir and add one-quarter of the prosciutto to the bowl. Microwave for 1 minute, or until cooked through.

Prep Ahead: This is a perfect recipe to make a single serving of at work. Just pack up the individual servings of veggies into a plastic bag and bring the eggs and prosciutto alongside them!

CHUNKY PALEO GRANOLA & FRUIT BOWL

Serves 4

Most meals are made ten times better when they have some kind of crunch to them and breakfast is no exception. I love eating this Paleo-approved granola plain right out of my hand, with almond milk and berries, over coconut yogurt or in a smoothie bowl!

Granola
½ cup (59 g) chopped walnuts
½ cup (54 g) slivered almonds
½ cup (70 g) raw cashews, chopped
¼ cup (37 g) almond flour
½ tsp salt
1 tbsp (3 g) chia seeds
1 tbsp (15 ml) melted coconut oil
1 tbsp (14 g) cashew butter
2 tbsp (30 ml) honey
1 tsp vanilla extract

Fruit
1 cup (166 g) chopped strawberries
1 cup (144 g) blackberries
1 medium banana, chopped

For Serving (optional)
Almond milk
Creamy Coconut Yogurt (page 108)

Preheat the oven to 350°F (175°C, or gas mark 4) and line a baking sheet with parchment paper. In a large bowl, combine the walnuts, almonds, cashews, almond flour, salt and chia seeds.

In another bowl, combine the coconut oil, cashew butter, honey and vanilla. Pour the wet ingredients over the nuts. Stir well to combine. Pour the mixture on the baking sheet and press into one even layer. It will look like one large cookie.

Bake for 13 to 15 minutes, or until lightly browned all over. Remove the granola from the oven and let it cool completely. Once cool, break the granola into small, bite-size pieces.

To serve, divide the granola into four bowls and top with some strawberries, blackberries and banana. Serve with almond milk or Creamy Coconut Yogurt (page 108), if desired.

Prep Ahead: Make the granola ahead of time and keep it in an airtight container in a cool, dry place for up to 2 weeks.

INSTANT POT® MACHACA BREAKFAST BURRITO BOWL

Serves 4

Machaca will always remind me of the night that Matt and I were on the hunt to find a place that served breakfast at dinnertime. We ended up at a Mexican restaurant, I got the machaca and eggs and my life was forever changed! If you aren't familiar with machaca, it is a spiced beef dish that is traditionally dried then rehydrated. And the Instant Pot makes it so flavorful and moist, there is no need for the long process!

Protein

2 tbsp (30 ml) avocado or olive oil, divided

½ medium yellow onion, chopped

1 tsp dried oregano

1 tsp cumin

1 tsp salt

1½ lb (680 g) chuck roast

1 tsp minced garlic

½ cup (120 ml) chicken broth

1 (8-oz [226-g]) can chopped tomatoes, drained

8 eggs

Salt and pepper

Veggies

1 tbsp (15 ml) avocado or olive oil

4 cups (400 g) cauliflower rice

4 cups (907 g) frozen hash browns

Salt and pepper

1 cup (240 ml) salsa

Protein

Place the Instant Pot on the sauté function and pour 1 tablespoon (15 ml) of the oil in the pot. Add the onion and stir to soften for 2 minutes. In a small bowl, combine the oregano, cumin and salt. Place the meat onto a plate and pour the spice mixture over the meat. Rub the spices all over the meat to coat it. Add the meat to the pot and brown it on all sides for 1 minute on each side.

Add the garlic and broth to the pot, then place the lid on top in the sealing position. Turn off the sauté function and turn it to manual, on high pressure for 60 minutes.

When it is done, switch the top knob to venting and once the pressure is released, take the meat out and shred it in a bowl. Add ½ cup (120 ml) of the liquid to the meat and then add the tomatoes.

Place a large skillet over medium heat and pour the remaining oil in the pan. In a bowl, crack the eggs and whisk them together with a pinch of salt and pepper. Pour them into the hot pan and scramble until cooked through.

Veggies

Place a large skillet over medium heat and pour the oil in the pan. Add the cauliflower rice to half the pan and hash browns to the other half. Let it cook for 2 minutes, then stir them together and season with salt and pepper. Cook for 3 to 5 minutes, or until tender.

To assemble the bowls, distribute the cauliflower mix evenly into four bowls and top each with some scrambled eggs, machaca beef and salsa.

Prep Ahead: Make the machaca beef up to 5 days before eating and reheat on the stovetop while everything else cooks.

SUPERFOOD-PACKED SMOOTHIE BOWL   Serves 4

A few years ago, we were living in a city where we could walk to the most amazing smoothie bowl place. It was SO good, and we went far too often considering the price! It wasn't until we finally got a good food processor that I realized I could make them at home exactly how I like them. This bowl has some hidden veggies so you aren't totally sugar bombed in the morning and can feel great about starting your day off right.

2 medium bananas, chopped and frozen★, plus 1 cup (118 g) fresh sliced banana

1 cup (149 g) frozen strawberries, plus 1 cup (116 g) fresh chopped strawberries

¾ cup (200 g) frozen pitaya (dragon fruit)

2 cups (264 g) frozen cauliflower rice

2 tbsp (14 g) flax meal

1½ cups (360 ml) unsweetened almond milk

2 tbsp (9 g) shredded coconut

1 tbsp (8 g) hemp hearts

2 cups (453 g) Chunky Paleo Granola (page 103)

Combine the frozen bananas, frozen strawberries, pitaya, cauliflower rice, flax meal and almond milk in a food processor or high-speed blender. Blend on high until smooth and creamy, about 4 to 6 minutes depending on how frozen the fruit is.

Pour into four bowls and top each with coconut, hemp hearts, fresh banana, fresh strawberries and Paleo granola!

★   Freeze the bananas in slices in a single layer so they don't stick together.

CREAMY COCONUT YOGURT BOWL

Serves 4

This breakfast is packed with nutrients and is such a fun project! I love the process of seeing simple coconut milk transform into creamy and thick yogurt in just a couple of days. If you are a yogurt lover and miss it while eating Paleo, you are going to flip over this dairy-free recipe!

1 (14-oz [415-ml]) can full-fat coconut milk

2 capsules probiotics

Chunky Paleo Granola (page 103)

Strawberry Compote (optional)

1 cup (149 g) frozen strawberries

2 tbsp (30 ml) orange juice

1 tsp vanilla extract

Place the closed can of coconut milk in a bowl of warm water for about 10 minutes to soften it. Shake vigorously, then pour it into a clean glass jar or bowl. Open the probiotic capsules into the coconut milk and use a wooden spoon (no metal) to stir them in and disperse them evenly. Cover the jar with cheesecloth or a thin tea towel, and secure it on top with a rubber band. Let it sit in a warm environment—by a window if the sun is shining, or near your stove—for 24 to 48 hours, then transfer it to the refrigerator.

You can eat the yogurt plain or make a strawberry compote to add more flavor. To make the strawberry compote, in a medium saucepan combine the frozen strawberries, orange juice and vanilla. Place the pan over medium heat and cook for 5 minutes until the strawberries break down. Transfer the compote to a bowl and place it in the fridge until cooled.

To make the yogurt bowl, scoop the coconut yogurt into a bowl and top it with strawberry compote (if using) and Chunky Paleo Granola (page 103).

Store the yogurt and compote in separate airtight containers in the refrigerator for up to 2 weeks.

BACON, DILL & SWEET POTATO BREAKFAST MASH

Serves 4

I have a love affair with sweet potatoes, and I don't care who knows it! Roast them, grill them, toast them or mash them—I am in. I once was on a SP kick where I just microwaved them whole and topped them with salsa and whatever meat was in the fridge. Not bad really, but I think you would be better off making this Paleo-friendly recipe instead!

Veggies

3 large sweet potatoes, peeled and chopped into 1-inch (2.5-cm) cubes

½ cup (120 ml) coconut milk

2 tbsp (28 g) ghee

2 tsp (2 g) chopped fresh dill

Salt and pepper

Protein

6 strips of bacon

4 eggs

Veggies

Place a large pot of water over high heat and bring to a boil. Add the sweet potatoes to the pot and boil them for about 8 minutes, or until fork tender. Remove them with a slotted spoon into a medium-sized bowl.

Add the coconut milk and ghee to the bowl. Mash the sweet potatoes with a potato masher or a fork until most of the lumps are gone. Add the fresh dill and stir to combine. Season to taste with salt and pepper.

Protein

While the sweet potatoes boil, place a large skillet over medium heat. Cook the bacon for about 5 minutes, flipping halfway through the cooking time, until the bacon is crispy. Remove from the pan and chop. Add the bacon to the sweet potato mash and stir to combine.

In that same pan with the bacon grease, add the eggs, making sure they don't touch. Fry the eggs until your desired yolk consistency is achieved.

To assemble the bowls, scoop the mash into four bowls and top each with a fried egg.

Prep Ahead: Make the sweet potato mash up to 5 days ahead of time and store it in the fridge. Reheat it in the microwave while your eggs and bacon cook.

PECAN PRALINE–SWEET POTATO MASH BOWL

My rule of thumb is usually to add bacon to all sweet potato concoctions, but that rule is waved when maple syrup and pecans are involved. Sweetened sweet potatoes have had a special place in my heart ever since my mom was sick one Thanksgiving and so I made our sweet potato casserole, this time loaded with marshmallows! This Paleo twist on sweet potatoes will put some pep in your step.

3 large sweet potatoes, peeled and chopped into 1-inch (2.5-cm) cubes

½ cup (120 ml) coconut milk

2 tbsp (30 ml) melted ghee

1 tsp cinnamon, divided

2 tbsp (30 ml) maple syrup

¾ tsp salt, divided

1 cup (109 g) chopped pecans

⅓ cup (66 g) coconut sugar, divided

2 tbsp (30 ml) water

Place a large pot of water over high heat and bring to a boil. Add the sweet potatoes to the pot and boil them for about 8 minutes, or until fork tender. Remove them with a slotted spoon into a medium-sized bowl.

Add the coconut milk and ghee to the bowl. Mash the sweet potatoes with a potato masher or a fork until most of the lumps are gone. Add ½ teaspoon of cinnamon, maple syrup and ½ teaspoon of salt. Stir to combine.

Place a medium skillet over medium heat. Add the pecans, about ¼ cup (54 g) of the coconut sugar, ½ teaspoon of cinnamon, ¼ teaspoon of salt and water to the pan. Toss to coat. Cook for 2 minutes until the sugar has dissolved and starts to boil, then cook for 2 minutes, stirring constantly.

Pour the pecans onto some parchment paper, spread them out, sprinkle with the remaining 1 tablespoon (12 g) of coconut sugar and let them cool.

To assemble the bowls, divide the mash among four bowls and top each with candied pecans.

Prep Ahead: Make the whole dish up to 5 days ahead of time and store in the fridge.

Amazing Appetizers & Snacks

This chapter is dedicated to two things I love: dips and coated fries. Is there anything else you could want in an appetizer or snack?

I don't know about you, but I love a good party: I love hosting a party. I love attending a party. And I especially love party food. I have some dips in here that are going to knock the socks off your guests. The Creamy Caramelized Onion Dip (page 117) and Chili Sweet Potato Fries (page 129) are sure to astonish all of your friends and family in the best way. You could make all of these dips and put them in separate bowls on one large board, then fill in all the open spaces with tons of chopped veggies and Paleo crackers. Thank goodness we live in an age when Paleo crackers and plantain chips are around every corner so we can get our snack on and feel great about it!

Loaded fries are another one of my favorite appetizers and the Paleo versions I made work with regular or sweet potatoes to please your pickiest eater.

These dips and fries are also my go-to snacks and now my daughter loves them too! I recommend making a dip or two at the beginning of the week, as well as cutting up some fresh veggies, so you always have a healthy snack option when the time comes. My Roasted Garlic Almond Dip (page 126) is almost always on hand in my fridge for a mid-afternoon snack.

CREAMY CARAMELIZED ONION DIP   Serves 4

This dip has been made more times than I can count already. It is everything I want in a dip, and I know you're going to love it. Here is a challenge: Bring this dip to a party and don't tell anyone what's in it. At the end of the night, shock everyone by saying "BOOM! It's dairy-free!!" They will go home flabbergasted and stomachache-free.

¾ cup (105 g) raw cashews, soaked in warm water for 2 to 8 hours

½ cup (120 ml) water

2 tbsp (28 g) ghee

2 medium yellow onions, diced

2 tbsp (30 ml) maple syrup

Salt and pepper

2 tbsp (8 g) chopped fresh parsley

1 tbsp (15 ml) coconut aminos

½ tsp garlic powder

For serving
Paleo crackers

Plantain chips

Drain the cashews and add them to a blender along with the ½ cup (120 ml) of water. Blend on high until creamy, about 1 to 2 minutes. Pour the mixture into a medium bowl.

Place a large skillet over medium-low heat and melt the ghee. Add the onions and cook, stirring occasionally, for about 5 minutes. Add the maple syrup and continue to cook for about 15 to 20 minutes, or until the onions are golden brown and fragrant. Season with salt and pepper.

Add the onions to the bowl of blended cashews along with the parsley, coconut aminos and garlic powder. Season the dip with salt and pepper to taste. Serve with paleo crackers (I like the Simple Mills brand) or plantain chips.

Prep Ahead: Make this up to 4 days ahead of time and store in the fridge.

COMFORTING CHICKEN POTPIE FRIES

Serves 4

When I think of comfort food, my brain goes immediately to chicken potpie. The best part is, all of the good flavors are in the filling, which can easily be made Paleo! Instead of pouring it into a puff pastry crust, I just poured it over oven-baked fries for a snack that you will want to eat with a fork.

3 medium russet potatoes

3 tbsp (45 ml) avocado or olive oil, divided

1 tsp salt, divided

½ lb (226 g) boneless, skinless chicken breasts

½ cup (120 ml) chicken broth

¼ cup (60 ml) coconut milk

½ tsp chopped thyme

½ tsp chopped rosemary

1 tsp arrowroot powder plus 1 tbsp (15 ml) water

½ cup (67 g) frozen peas

½ cup (64 g) chopped carrots

Preheat the oven to 400°F (200°C, or gas mark 6). Line two baking sheets with parchment paper. Peel the potatoes and slice them into fries, then divide them between the two baking sheets. Pour 1 tablespoon (15 ml) of oil and ½ teaspoon salt over each pan and toss to coat. Bake for 40 minutes, tossing halfway through.

To make the topping, place a large skillet over medium heat. Pour the remaining 1 tablespoon (15 ml) of oil in the pan followed by the chicken breasts. Cook for 3 to 4 minutes per side until done, then remove the chicken from the pan and set it aside.

To the same pan, pour in the broth and coconut milk and add the thyme and rosemary. Bring it to a boil, then add the arrowroot mixture while stirring vigorously. Chop the chicken and add it to the sauce, followed by the peas and carrots. Cook for 3 to 4 minutes, until the peas are defrosted and the carrots have softened slightly.

When the fries are done baking, serve them in a bowl topped with the chicken potpie mixture.

Prep Ahead: The chicken potpie topping can be made up to 4 days ahead of time, reheated and poured on fresh fries.

ASIAN ALMOND DIP   Serves 4

I really just love an almond dip. It is the kind of thing I make and seriously wonder how it isn't as popular in the world as hummus and ranch. With just some soaking time for the almonds and a quick blend in the food processor, this dip is great as a snack, in a salad or watered down with an additional ¼ cup (60 ml) of water and drizzled on lettuce wraps!

1 cup (138 g) unsalted roasted almonds, soaked for 4 to 12 hours

½ cup (120 ml) water

3 tbsp (45 ml) sesame oil

3 tbsp (45 ml) coconut aminos

2 tbsp (5 g) nutritional yeast

2 tsp (6 g) minced garlic

1 tsp garlic powder

1 tsp ground ginger

½ tsp onion powder

1 tsp salt, plus more to taste

For Serving

Bell pepper slices

Snap peas

Carrots

Drain the soaked almonds and add them to a food processor. Add the fresh water, sesame oil, coconut aminos, nutritional yeast, garlic, garlic powder, ginger, onion powder and salt. Blend on high for 2 to 3 minutes, until the almonds have broken down completely and the dip is relatively smooth.

Season to taste with salt and blend again. Serve this dip with sliced bell peppers, snap peas and carrots.

Prep Ahead: Make this up to 1 week ahead of time and store it in the fridge.

FIESTA GUACAMOLE

Serves 4

It is my firm belief that everyone needs a standard and delicious guacamole recipe in their repertoire, so I am here to fill that need for you! Garlic, lime and salt are the must-haves, but I also love a little red onion crunch. This guac goes well on so many bowls in this book, but it's tasty enough to eat with carrot chips too!

4 ripe avocados, pitted and peeled
½ cup (80 g) diced red onion
1 tsp minced garlic
½ tsp garlic powder
1 tbsp (15 ml) lime juice
Salt

For Serving
Sliced carrots
Sliced bell pepper
Sliced cucumber

In a medium bowl, combine the avocados, onion, garlic, garlic powder and lime juice. Mash the avocados with a fork and stir to combine them with the other ingredients. Season with salt to taste. Serve with sliced raw veggies.

Prep Ahead: If prepping guacamole ahead of time, pour it into an airtight container and pour a thin layer of cold water over the top. When it's time to serve, pour the water off, stir and enjoy.

CREAMY SWEET POTATO & CAULIFLOWER HUMMUS

I love a good array of appetizers at a party, and dips are just the best. Hummus made with chickpeas is a classic, but it can leave your stomach feeling less than awesome. This version is made with sweet potatoes and cauliflower, and it has all the tasty flavor of your standard hummus. I love this version in the fall because the color is so beautiful for the season!

1 large sweet potato, peeled and chopped

2 cups (200 g) cauliflower florets

¼ cup (60 ml) tahini

2 tbsp (30 ml) olive oil

2 tbsp (30 ml) lemon juice

1 tsp minced garlic

Salt

For Serving
Sliced vegetables
Paleo crackers

Place a large pot of water over high heat and bring it to a boil. Add the sweet potato and cauliflower florets to the pot and cook for 8 minutes, or until both are fork tender. Drain the veggies, then add them to a food processor.

Add the tahini, oil, lemon juice and garlic to the food processor and blend until smooth. Season with salt to taste. Scoop the dip into a bowl. Serve with veggies and Paleo crackers.

Prep Ahead: Make this dip up to 5 days ahead of time and store it in the fridge.

ROASTED GARLIC ALMOND DIP   Serves 4

Remember how earlier in this book I said I loved garlic? Well, roasted garlic actually takes the #1 spot. The flavor is all of the good parts of garlic with the bitterness taken out and with a bit of a sweet flavor added. So, of course, we had to roast up a whole head of garlic and throw it in our favorite almond dip!

1 bulb of garlic

¼ cup (60 ml) avocado or olive oil, divided

Salt

1 cup (143 g) unsalted roasted almonds, soaked in water for 4 to 12 hours

½ cup (120 ml) water

2 tbsp (30 ml) coconut aminos

2 tbsp (12 g) nutritional yeast

2 tsp (6 g) garlic powder

1 tsp onion powder

For Serving
Paleo crackers
Sliced vegetables

Preheat the oven to 400°F (200°C, or gas mark 6). Slice off the top of a bulb of garlic so that some of the cloves are exposed and place the garlic bulb on a piece of foil. Drizzle with 1 tablespoon (15 ml) of oil and a pinch of salt, then wrap up the bulb with foil. Place that in the oven for 30 minutes so the garlic gets nice and soft.

Once the roasted garlic is cool enough to handle, squeeze from the bottom of the bulb to get out all of the roasted garlic. Set it aside.

Drain the almonds and add them to a food processor. Add the fresh water, 3 tablespoons (45 ml) of oil, coconut aminos, nutritional yeast, garlic powder and onion powder. Blend on high for 3 to 5 minutes, or until smooth. Season to taste with salt.

Serve with Paleo crackers and veggies!

Prep Ahead: Make this up to 1 week ahead of time and store it in the fridge.

CHILI SWEET POTATO FRIES

Serves 4

Sweet potatoes, I've loved you for so long, I decided to write you a song.
You taste so good with chili or just salt. You are my side dish default.
I sometimes call you sweet taters. I wish I could hug your creators.

If this poem doesn't get you to crave this dish, just think about the crispiness of the sweet potato fries covered with a chili mixture so packed with flavor that you won't be able to stop eating them! Great for an afternoon snack for the family or a football party, this appetizer never disappoints.

Veggies

4 large sweet potatoes, peeled and chopped into fries
3 tbsp (45 ml) avocado or olive oil
1 tsp salt
½ tsp garlic powder

Meat

1 tbsp (15 ml) avocado or olive oil
1 lb (454 g) ground beef
1 (14.5-oz [411-g]) can diced, fire-roasted tomatoes
3 tbsp (48 g) tomato paste
⅓ cup (80 ml) water
2 tsp (5 g) chili powder
1 tsp garlic powder
½ tsp paprika
Salt and pepper
Chopped parsley

Veggies

Preheat the oven to 425°F (220°C, or gas mark 7). Line two baking sheets with parchment paper and place the sweet potatoes on one sheet. Pour the oil over the sweet potatoes and toss to coat. Sprinkle with salt and garlic powder. Toss again. Divide the sweet potato fries between the two baking sheets and lay them in one even layer.

Bake the fries for 20 minutes. Flip them and cook for another 15 to 20 minutes, or until crispy.

Meat

While the fries cook, place a large skillet over medium heat. Pour the oil in the pan followed by the beef. Cook the beef for 5 to 7 minutes, breaking it up as it cooks. Add the tomatoes, tomato paste, water, chili powder, garlic powder and paprika. Stir, cooking for 5 minutes to thicken. Season with salt and pepper to taste.

To assemble the appetizer bowl, place all of the fries in a serving bowl and top with the chili and parsley. Share with friends!

BACON-WRAPPED DATE DIP

Serves 4

I have a deep love for bacon-wrapped dates. How could you not?! They are a sweet and salty match made in heaven. So, because this is a bowl book, I had to figure out how I could make my favorite appetizer into dip. And friends, I did it! With a base of creamy cashews and sweet dates, this dip will make your friends love you even more.

½ cup (70 g) raw cashews

1½ cups (284 g) Medjool dates

¾ cup (180 ml) water

5 slices bacon

1 cup (160 g) chopped onion

Salt and pepper

For Serving

Paleo crackers

Plantain chips

In a medium bowl, combine the cashews and dates. Bring about 3 cups (720 ml) of water to a boil in a teapot. Pour boiling water over the cashews and dates so they are covered and soak them for 30 to 60 minutes.

Once soaked, drain the cashews and dates. Add them to a blender along with the fresh water and blend on high until smooth and creamy. Set it aside.

Place a large skillet over medium heat. Once the pan is hot, cook the bacon for 2 minutes per side until crispy. Remove the bacon from the pan and add the onion to the bacon grease. Cook the onion for about 5 minutes, or until soft. Chop the bacon.

In a bowl, combine the creamy cashew mixture with the cooked onion and bacon. Season to taste with salt and pepper and serve with Paleo crackers or plantain chips.

Prep Ahead: Make this up to 5 days ahead of time and store in the fridge.

Satisfying Sweets

I eat dessert every day. It is the thing I love and if I let myself eat it every day, I never need to gorge on something crazy sweet and huge. If no food is "forbidden," then there is no need to get all worked up about needing a large ice cream on your way home from work or a cinnamon roll at the airport.

When switching to a more Paleo-based diet, it can seem like all you can eat are veggies and meat, but don't despair! Thanks to great advancements in grain-free and refined sugar–free products, there are so many options at the store to put together some desserts you will love. Using natural sweeteners and alternative flours, such as almond flour and cassava flour, has made eating clean so much easier. It satisfies my sweet tooth on a daily basis.

This chapter is packed with everything from a Microwave Double Chocolate Cake Bowl (page 136) to a Salted Caramel Banana Nice Cream (page 143) that you are going to have to fight your family for. And because you know I like a party, all of these can be made in large batches and shared with everyone at the end of the night. If this chapter isn't a clear solution to having your (clean eating) cake and eating it too, I don't know what is!

CREAMY VANILLA BEAN BERRYLICIOUS BOWL

When people say eat fruit for dessert, I get a little upset. Yes, it's sweet. But is it really satisfying your sweet tooth?! Well, it is if you pour a creamy vanilla sauce all over a bowl of berries! This sauce is great to have on hand when you need a sweet treat without a sugar overload.

½ cup (70 g) raw cashews, soaked in hot water for 2 to 8 hours

¼ cup (60 ml) maple syrup

½ cup (120 ml) water

Pinch of salt

1 vanilla bean

4 cups (492 g) chopped strawberries and blueberries

Drain cashews then add them to a blender with the maple syrup, fresh water and a pinch of salt. Blend on high until smooth, about 1 minute. Slice a vanilla bean down the middle and scrape out the beans inside. Add them to the mixture and blend for a few seconds.

To serve, add strawberries and blueberries to the bowls. Pour the vanilla cream over them.

Prep Ahead: Make the vanilla bean sauce up to 1 week ahead of time and store in the fridge.

MICROWAVE DOUBLE CHOCOLATE CAKE BOWL

Serves 4

Do you ever crave cake after dinner and end up sad because there is no cake? Same. Luckily, I made you this simple Paleo cake recipe that you cook individually in the microwave! No need to wait for preheating or having your oven heat up your house. This recipe is everything your cake-loving self needs, and it uses cassava flour, which is made from a root and works perfectly in Paleo baking!

3 large eggs

2 tsp (10 ml) vanilla extract

¼ cup (60 ml) melted coconut oil

¼ cup (60 ml) maple syrup

⅓ cup (94 g) cashew butter

½ cup (64 g) cassava flour★

¼ cup (25 g) cacao powder

1 tsp baking powder

Pinch of salt

¼ cup (57 g) chocolate chips, plus more for garnish

Coconut whipped cream★★

In a medium bowl, combine the eggs, vanilla, coconut oil, maple syrup and cashew butter. Add the cassava flour, cacao powder, baking powder, salt and chocolate chips.

Divide the batter among four small, microwave-safe bowls. Microwave the bowls one at a time for 1 minute and 20 seconds.

Top with coconut whipped cream and additional chocolate chips.

★ Cassava Flour: This Paleo flour is made from the cassava root. It is a great alternative in baking, because it is nut-free but has a slightly nutty flavor and a smooth texture.

★ ★ Coconut whipped cream can be found in most health food stores, or you can use any non-dairy whipped cream you find.

COOKIE DOUGH DIP

Serves 4

Favorite cookie, 1, 2, 3, GO! For me, it will always and forever be a classic chocolate chip. I also happen to love the dough because I am a normal human like that. In this recipe, I took all the goodness of cookie dough and made it into a dip using a base of cashews to keep it grain-free and packed with protein, so it's refined and fancy. Dip Paleo cookies in it if you want to be awesome, or fruit if you know you will probably eat the whole bowl.

1 cup (140 g) raw cashews, soaked in warm water for 2 to 8 hours

½ cup (120 ml) almond milk

¼ cup (37 g) almond flour

1 tbsp (7 g) coconut flour

1 tsp vanilla extract

¼ cup (50 g) coconut sugar

¼ cup (57 g) mini chocolate chips

For Serving (optional)
Strawberries
Apples
Paleo cookies

Drain the cashews and add them to a blender with the almond milk, almond flour, coconut flour and vanilla. Blend on high until creamy, about 1 to 2 minutes. Pour the mixture into a bowl, and stir in the coconut sugar and chocolate chips.

Serve with strawberries, apples, Paleo cookies or a spoon!

Prep Ahead: Make this up to 1 week ahead of time and store in the fridge.

GERMAN CHOCOLATE CAKE DIP Serves 4

If you are a German chocolate cake fan, get ready to flip out over this dip. The base is a smooth, chocolatey dip topped with a sweet coconut and pecan filling that will bring back all the memories. To make the topping just like the creamy original, I used a mixture of dates, honey and coconut milk—all natural and all delicious!

Dip

1 cup (140 g) raw cashews
½ cup (120 ml) water
¼ cup (57 g) chocolate chips
1 tbsp (14 g) coconut oil
1 tbsp (12 g) cacao powder
1 tbsp (7 g) coconut flour
¼ cup (60 ml) honey
½ tsp vanilla extract
Pinch of salt

Topping

½ cup (114 g) pitted Medjool dates
2 tbsp (30 ml) honey
2 tbsp (27 g) coconut oil
3 tbsp (45 ml) coconut milk
2 tbsp (9 g) shredded coconut
2 tbsp (22 g) chopped pecans

For Serving

Fresh fruit
Paleo cookies

Dip

Place the cashews in a bowl, cover them with warm water and soak for 2 to 8 hours. Drain the cashews and add them to a blender along with the fresh water. Blend on high until creamy, about 1 to 2 minutes.

In a small, microwave-safe bowl, combine the chocolate chips and coconut oil. Microwave that for 30 seconds, or until melted. Stir and add the mixture to the blender with the cashews. Add the cacao powder, coconut flour, honey, vanilla and a pinch of salt. Blend on high until smooth.

Topping

In a food processor, combine the pitted Medjool dates, honey, coconut oil and coconut milk. Blend until the dates break down and are smooth. Add the coconut and pecans and pulse a few times to combine.

Place the chocolate cake dip in a bowl and top it with the coconut-pecan mixture. Serve with fruit or Paleo cookies.

Prep Ahead: Make the chocolate dip and topping up to 5 days ahead of time and store them separately in the fridge.

SALTED CARAMEL BANANA NICE CREAM

Serves 4

The simple pleasure of banana nice cream has been upgraded in this salted caramel version! This book would not be complete without a frozen treat, so get ready to stock your freezer with this stuff all summer long. If you miss the creamy texture of ice cream while eating dairy-free, then nice cream will satisfy that craving perfectly!

4 ripe bananas
1 cup (227 g) pitted Medjool dates
1 tsp vanilla extract
½ tsp salt

Line a baking sheet with parchment paper. Peel and slice the bananas and lay the slices on the sheet. Place the sliced bananas in the freezer and freeze for at least 4 hours, or until frozen.

When the bananas are frozen, place the Medjool dates in a small bowl and cover them with warm water. Let the dates soak for 10 to 20 minutes, then drain.

Remove the bananas from the freezer and add them to a food processor along with the dates, vanilla and salt. Blend on high for 2 to 4 minutes, or until smooth.

Prep Ahead: Make this up to 2 weeks ahead of time and store in the freezer.

DATE CARAMEL APPLE DIP

Serves 4

I have vivid memories of chowing down on apples dipped in caramel sauce or getting my teeth stuck to caramel apple lollipops as a kid. The flavor combination is so delicious, and it had been way too long since I enjoyed those flavors without a serious sugar hangover. So, I created this delicious dessert bowl and it totally takes me back! Sweetened with dates and maple syrup, and made nice and creamy by the cashews, you will love this throwback.

½ cup (70 g) raw cashews
6 Medjool dates, pitted
¼ cup (60 ml) maple syrup
½ cup (120 ml) water
Pinch of salt
4 medium apples, cored and sliced

Place cashews in a bowl and cover them with hot water. Let the cashews soak for 2 to 8 hours, then drain them.

In a blender, combine the soaked cashews, dates, maple syrup, fresh water and a pinch of salt. Blend on high until smooth, about 1 minute.

Pour the dip into a bowl and serve with apple slices.

Prep Ahead: Make this up to 5 days ahead of time and store in the fridge.

Acknowledgments

We did it! I don't think I could ever take full credit for this book being in your hands because so many people supported me to make this happen.

To my sweet husband Matt, thank you for being my #1 taste tester and support system. When I was stressed about getting this book made and perfected, you held my hand the whole way, keeping our daughter entertained when I ran to a coffee shop, or by doing . . . all the laundry. I love you so much, and this book is here because of you!

To my adorable girl Ruthie, you motivate me so much every day to keep things light and happy with your infectious smile. I could never thank you enough for all you have done to my life!

To my mom, dad and sisters, Brittany and Taylor, thank you for being my original taste-testing team and always supporting my crazy ventures. Your constant love for me, the baby of the fam, goes deep into my core and I feel it every day!

To Catherine, my teammate in creating this book, there is no doubt it would never have happened without you! Between your fabulous contributions in recipe development to your measurement conversion skills, this book is absolutely yours, too.

To my amazing publisher Page Street, thank you for supporting my ideas and punny title! I'm honored to be a published author because of you!

And to all of my readers who flipped out when I told them I got a book deal and have been supportive of me my entire blogging career—this book would not exist without you!

About the Author

Kelsey Preciado is the writer and photographer behind the blog Little Bits of Real Food, as well as a mother to Ruthie and wife to Matt. Her whole life has been spent loving to cook and share meals with loved ones. In 2015, Kelsey first began to cut out processed foods and eat a more whole-food diet, and it completely changed the way she felt. Using her knowledge in the kitchen, Kelsey was able to develop healthy recipes that swept the internet, leading to her being featured on *The Dr. Oz Show*, in *Glamour* magazine as well as in many online publications such as People, Well + Good and BuzzFeed.

When she's not cooking or on Instagram, you can find her dancing with her family or splashing in the pool with them! Living in Southern California, she is always trying to get outside and soak up the sunshine.

Index